Napoleon's
Hemorrhoids

Napoleon's Hemorrhoids

. . . AND OTHER SMALL EVENTS THAT CHANGED HISTORY

PHIL MASON

A Herman Graf Book
Skyhorse Publishing

Skyhorse Publishing books may be purchased in bulk at special
discounts for sales promotion, corporate gifts, fund-raising, or
educational purposes. Special editions can also be created to
specifications. For details, contact the Special Sales Department,
Skyhorse Publishing, 555 Eighth Avenue, Suite 903,
New York, NY 10018 or info@skyhorsepublishing.com.

www.skyhorsepublishing.com

10 9 8 7 6 5 4 3 2

Paperback ISBN: 978-1-61608-132-4

Library of Congress Cataloging-in-Publication Data

Mason, Phil, 1958-
Napoleon's hemorrhoids : and other small events that changed history /
Phil Mason.
p. cm.
Includes index.
ISBN 978-1-60239-764-4
1. World history--Anecdotes. 2. History--Anecdotes. 3. World
history--Anecdotes. I. Title.
D24.M36 2009
909--dc22
2009022969

Printed in the United States of America

Contents

For Phillip – our very own tiny event that changed this household forever, and without whose constant support and encouragement this book would have been finished in half the time.
(with apologies to PGW)

INTRODUCTION

This is a book about tiny events. Tiny events that had big impacts. Some changed the world. Some changed individuals' lives and their contribution to the world. Some would have changed the world if matters had turned out just a little differently.

Napoleon's attack of piles on the morning of the Battle of Waterloo is said to have prevented him from his usual practice of keeping a watchful eye on progress by riding vigorously around the battlefield. Instead, on that morning he was acutely discomfited, a shadow of his usual self. He was distracted, failed to issue clear orders and delayed commencing hostilities until 11.20am, more than five hours after originally intended. He was eventually to be scuppered in the early evening by the last-gasp arrival of Allied reinforcements in the shape of the Prussians, which leads to the intriguing thought that the tussle might have been over well before they reached the battlefield had Napoleon been his usual driven self.

The Duke of Wellington, who led the winning side that day, famously acknowledged that the encounter had been 'the closest run thing you ever saw in your life.' To his brother on the day after the battle, he wrote, 'It was the most desperate business I was ever in. I never took so much trouble about any battle and never was so near being beat.' So it is entirely conceivable that had Napoleon's hemorrhoids not intervened just at the wrong time, the outcome of Waterloo and the future of Europe could well have turned out very differently.

*

Welcome to the world of 'if only' and 'what if'. This is history with a twist. *Napoleon's Hemorrhoids* tells the tales of how small turns of chance, accident and fate had bigger impacts on the course of history than might have been expected. How Adolf Hitler would have committed suicide years before he ever got near the reaches of power in Germany but for the intervention of a family friend. How the shape of British politics was moulded by a foreign king who couldn't speak the language and a queen who, despite giving birth nineteen times, couldn't leave an heir. How Churchill narrowly escaped with his life three times before becoming Britain's salvation in the Second World War. How Harold Wilson triumphed at the polls by forcing a change to the timing of a television programme. And how there may never have been a Thatcher era had Jim Callaghan not bottled out of calling an election in 1978. Or a Reagan era had his attempt to join the Communist Party when he was 27 not been thwarted because the Communists deemed him to be too dim.

The impression of history we get from our schoolteachers and our history books is one of logical progression and reason. Things happen for a reason. Big things happen for big reasons. *Napoleon's Hemorrhoids* explodes this myth. Much of history turns out to be the consequence of small acts of fortune, accident or luck, good or bad.

Great sweeps of history boil down to small moments of chance. We see how the Spanish Armada failed to invade in 1588 despite the British fleet running out of ammunition and sinking just one enemy ship. How the most decisive battle of the American Civil War – Gettysburg – was fought by accident. How a doctor's misdiagnosis can be held to have indirectly led to the First World War. How a driver's wrong turn and a chance cup of coffee led to the assassination that did spark the conflict.

We see how Germany was told early on in the Second World War that the Allies had broken their famed Enigma code, but they couldn't bring themselves to believe it possible so carried on using the penetrated system. How weather forecasters almost cancelled the D-Day landings in favour of a later date, which would have brought catastrophe. How during the Cuban missile crisis American and Soviet planes were just two and a half minutes away from opening fire. How Britain's nuclear tests almost took place in Lincolnshire.

Significant decisions that have had historic and lasting impact have turned on the smallest of matters. We see how the Panama Canal was nearly built in Nicaragua but for a postage stamp, and how the United Nations headquarters was headed for Philadelphia until a last minute land deal secured it for New York, and for possibly the least charitable of reasons. How the first to climb Everest shouldn't have been Hillary and Tenzing. How Kennedy shouldn't have been elected president in the first place, and how his womanising just before the fateful day in Dallas directly contributed to his death. How Nixon's White House taping system which caused his downfall in the Watergate scandal was revealed by an aide accidentally. And how the 76-year-old Ronald Reagan would have been removed from office by his staff had he shown any signs of incapacity on one particular day in 1987 – he happened to be on good form that day, and survived being deposed.

We also cover the worlds of science, arts, sport and business. Each field is replete with instances of major achievement deriving from the smallest of beginnings. How a vast array of inventions came by pure chance. How the introduction of train travel in Britain rested on a lie to Parliament by George Stephenson. How Charles Darwin nearly did not get his trip on the *Beagle* because of the shape of his nose. How Alexander Graham Bell deceived his way to recognition as the inventor of the telephone. How one of the world's greatest nuclear scientists became a physicist only because he lined up in the wrong queue at university. And how nearly every moon mission scraped through mission-threatening disasters.

In the field of arts, we witness some of the greatest cultural achievements of history emerging from unexpected origins. How the world's most successful film nearly wasn't made. And how it was based on one of the world's highest-selling books that was only written because the author broke her ankle and had to rest up. How the scene voted 'the coolest in cinema history' was entirely ad-libbed because the lead actor was suffering from diarrhoea and was unable to perform the elaborate fight scene that was scripted. We see how celebrated actors secured by chance the parts that made them famous, and others who turned them down. And how many of literature's most renowned works were the result of the smallest and least planned inspirations.

In sport, we find stories of individual success – and failure – through small but decisive turns of fate. Don Bradman, the best cricketer there's ever been, who needed just four runs in his last innings to end his Test career on an average of 100, being bowled for nought second ball. Hanif Mohammad setting a record individual score but discovering, because the scoreboard was wrong, that he had run himself out on 499, when he was hoping to surpass the magical mark of 500. How major sporting events have been decided because umpires have been looking the other way, having tea or getting ice creams. And how the Russians arrived late at one early Olympics because they forgot they were on a different calendar.

We see how some of the most successful and lasting commercial ventures were born not of planning and considered homework but sudden inspiration by a chance experience or insight. McDonald's would not have become a global phenomenon had a marketing man not wondered why he was being asked to supply 40 milkshake makers to an apparently too small retail outfit. The credit card might not have evolved if the founder of the idea had not forgotten his wallet. The ubiquitous modern PIN number might not have been four numbers if the creator's wife had had a better memory. And we see how some of the world's most popular and enduring games were initially judged to be complete failures and won success through chance.

In the world of chance beginnings, the Spitfire might have been named the Shrike or the Shrew had it not been for the designer overhearing a blazing row between the company chairman and his daughter. One of the world's most famous books was written for a bet that one could not be written using just 50 different words. And one of the world's most successful television adverts was inspired by an executive being stranded, fogbound, in an Irish airport terminal.

Along, we hope, with intriguing you with how the world around us today might have been very different had tiny acts of chance not intervened, *Napoleon's Hemorrhoids* will cure you of two misconceptions. Firstly, that history is relentlessly boring. Far from it, as what follows, I trust, shows. And secondly, that significant historical events have to be produced by significant and great causes.

It may sometimes be a source of comfort to believe that the course of history – and our destiny – is firmly guided by important decision-makers making their decisions for important reasons. For those who believe this, reading what follows may cause some alarm. Be aware, not everything that happens does so for a good, or even decently sized, reason.

Read on, be amused, be amazed. And for those who would still rather believe in the comfort of the school-book version of how history unfolds, be a little afraid.

Phil Mason

1

Detours on the March
of History

**According to University of Pennsylvania anthropologist
Solomon Katz**, the transformation of early humans from their
wandering hunter-gatherer lifestyle to settled farming, the
fundamental change that allowed cities and civilisation to develop,
was caused by the accidental discovery of...beer.

In March 1987, Katz published his theory that some 10,000 years
ago in Mesopotamia, Neolithic Sumerian man accidentally discovered that wheat and barley, when soaked in water to make
gruel, did not rot if it was left in the open air but instead, through
natural yeast, turned into a frothy brew which not only altered a
drinker's mood but provided significant sustenance. It was second
only to animal protein as a source of nutrition.

Katz based his theory on the discovery that the earliest recipe
found in Sumerian culture is a tablet describing how to make beer.
The mood-altering effects, according to Katz, would have been a
strong incentive to begin sowing and growing the grains.

'The initial discovery of a stable way to make alcohol provided
enormous motivation for continuing to collect these seeds,' said
Katz. He contended that early man would have needed a strong
reason to move away from the hunting life which provided a much
more reliable standard of living than back-breaking agriculture.
Had beer not produced the elevating effects it did, man might

1

never have made the shift to settling down into static communities, the bedrock of all human civilisation that has followed.

In one of the ironies of history, it was a Roman Catholic pope who originally granted rule over Ireland to the English.

Alexander III, wanting to eradicate pagan Irish customs which conflicted with Catholic teaching, issued a declaration at the Synod of Cashel in 1172 recognising English King Henry II as Lord of Ireland and authorising its occupation.

For seven hundred years during the critical period of growth of the Roman church, the entire religious authority of the popes rested on a not-so-clever forgery. It was not until the Middle Ages that the ruse was exposed, by which time the church had successfully consolidated itself.

To support its position as the spiritual ruler of the continent at a time when Rome faced increasing challenge from other emerging kingdoms, the papal court relied on the 'Donation of Constantine', a grant of lands and political and religious supremacy supposedly made in 315 by Constantine the Great, the first Roman Emperor to convert to Christianity, to the then pope, Sylvester. It conferred upon the popes recognition of their supremacy in all religious matters in the Roman Empire's four great sees, Antioch, Jerusalem, Alexandria and Constantinople, and granted Sylvester and his successors 'Rome and all the provinces, districts and cities of Italy and the West as subject to the Roman church for ever.'

It went on to purport that Constantine – then based in the later Empire's eastern seat in what would become Constantinople – had decided to site himself there because it would not be right for him to be located in the city where the head of the Christian faith reigned.

The supposed donation was not revealed publicly until the

2

mid-700s when it was used in 754 by Pope Stephen to negotiate with Frankish King Pepin about the division of lands between the two rival authorities. It was wheeled out again in 1054 when Leo IX was in dispute with the patriarch of Constantinople over the rights and powers of Roman rule. It became an essential document in later years as popes reacted to challenges against their authority in the growing post-Dark Age Europe in the 10th and 11th centuries.

It was, though, entirely fictitious. Thought now to have been concocted by the papal chancery to provide retrospective authority for the increasingly strained church, it was not until the 15th century, nearly 700 years after its appearance, that scholars began openly questioning its veracity. It was finally debunked in 1518.

It should have been easy. One of the giveaways to the forgery was Constantine's apparent bequeathing of his own city to papal spiritual control. Although supposedly written in 315, Constantine did not in fact found Constantinople until 326, 11 years *after* his apparent donation.

Marco Polo's discoveries in China were only recorded for posterity because he found himself spending a year in a Genoan jail with an inquisitive cell mate.

He had been captured in 1298 while serving as an honorary master of a Venetian vessel, fighting one of the sporadic wars with the rival trading state of Genoa. He was persuaded to document his twenty-two-year exploits in the Far East by his cell mate, Rustichello da Pisa, who took down the explorer's memoirs and published them.

The *Travels of Marco Polo* revealed to the European world the hitherto unknown civilisations of Tibet, China, Mongolia and Siam (present day Thailand). It also contained the first mention in Europe of China's formidable technological advantage, in areas such as block printing, paper money and coal-fired technologies.

Marco Polo was, without doubt, an industrious and resourceful traveller, but the world would only find out about it because he turned out to be a rather less accomplished naval commander.

Columbus very nearly failed to discover America. He came within a day of having to abandon his first voyage to the New World in 1492, despite his subterfuge to deceive his crew as to how far they were actually travelling.

He kept two logs, a true one for his reckoning and a false one to show his men so they would not be alarmed at the vast distance they were, in fact, covering. He would never have got as far as he did without the deception. Still, on 9 October, after 67 days at sea, amidst an increasingly fraught atmosphere, he was forced to promise his restless party that if land was not sighted within three days, he would turn back for home. On the morning of the third day, 12 October, his lookout announced landfall.

If you have ever wondered why, since Columbus 'discovered' America, it does not bear his name, it is because of a fake travelogue, an error made by a mapmaker and Columbus's refusal to his dying day to accept that he had not in fact reached Asia.

Five years after Columbus's first voyage, Florentine navigator, Amerigo Vespucci, repeated the feat, this time to what is now known as South America, and he did declare for the first time that this was a separate continent.

He never intended or aspired to have the New World named after him. He became associated entirely by accident. A forger, after a quick buck, fabricated letters purporting to be Vespucci's reports home of the new places he had discovered. One of these fake letters was seen 10 years later by a mapmaker, Martin Waldseemuller, who was preparing a new atlas. He wrote in the margin of his depiction of the New World, in Latin, that he thought it should be called after Americus (the Latin form of

Amerigo) 'or America, as both Europe and Asia had the feminine form of name.'

The map of the New World was published and what is now Brazil was christened 'Americus'. When the celebrated cartographer Mercator produced his first maps, the tag had spread to the whole of the continent, North and South. By then Vespucci was dead, completely unaware that he had given his name to an entire new world.

New York became British because of a Dutch obsession with nutmegs. When a British adventurer and trader, Nathaniel Courthope, seized the tiny island of Pulo Run in the Spice Islands (near Java in what is modern Indonesia) in 1616, he disrupted the Dutch monopoly of the area and the lucrative spice trade which reaped gargantuan profits. A pennyworth of nutmeg bought there could be sold for 600 times that amount back in Europe. The Dutch recovered Pulo Run just four years later, but not before Courthope had got the island's chieftains to sign a formal treaty of alliance with Britain.

Half a century later, when the British and Dutch were negotiating the peace treaty of Breda, the Dutch agreed to buy out the alliance by trading another of its colonies which it saw as having no value. For Pulo Run and its nutmegs, it swapped a then rather desolate island in America – Manhattan.

The birth of the Reformation – the religious upheaval that split Christianity into Protestant and Catholic sects – can trace its origins to its founder's chronic constipation. Martin Luther, who famously composed his 95 theses protesting against the abuses of the papacy and nailed them to a church door in Wittenburg in 1517, regularly complained in his writings of his suffering and that he spent much of his time in solitary contemplation on the toilet.

Historians have long noted the strong lavatorial allusions that fill Luther's work. He records having his revelatory inspiration '*in cloaca*', Latin for 'in the sewer', and he frequently used barbed language to vent his frustration ('I shit on the Devil' and 'I break wind on the Devil') some of which was clearly not only theological.

He wrote that his major doctrinal insight, which would change world history, was 'knowledge the Holy Spirit gave me on the privy in the tower.' The theses themselves may well have been drafted there too as he sat through the long quiet hours on the lavatory. It is also perhaps now easier to understand why there were so many of them.

Archaeologists excavating a disused annex of Luther's house in Wittenburg in 2004 uncovered a brick alcove which they believed to be the actual toilet. It was a comfortable, 18-inch square seat with plumbing said to be of a quality quite advanced for its time.

Louis XVI and his queen, Marie Antoinette, might have avoided execution during the French Revolution had the queen not changed their escape plans at the last minute. In June 1791, two years after the outbreak of revolution, with the government descending into anarchy and the chances of a constitutional monarchy evaporating, Louis had decided to flee Paris for the nearest border – modern Belgium – 200 miles away, where royalist allies would help him into exile.

The original plan had been for Louis to leave alone in a quick, small carriage. Marie, however, when the time came to separate, insisted that they travel together. That required a larger coach and made it a slower journey – barely seven miles an hour.

The pair left the Louvre at night, separately to avoid suspicion. Marie then got lost in the maze of the Tuileries Gardens for half an hour before she caught up with the king.

The slower pace, and a broken wheel which had to be fixed, meant that by late afternoon the next day they were three hours behind schedule for the rendezvous with their armed guard who were due to meet them en route. The guards, suspecting that the plan had misfired, had by then decided to disperse.

The escape party arrived at the small village of Sainte-Menehould where they stopped to change horses. News had already spread of their flight, and the postmaster recognised the king, according to many accounts, by checking his face against the royal image printed on a 50-livre banknote. As the escapees left, so did he and he overtook them to warn the authorities in the next main town, Varennes.

The royal pair were apprehended there, only 25 miles from safety, returned to Paris in ignominy and 18 months later Louis was guillotined, with Marie following nine months later.

A Cambridge professor put forward a theory in 2000 that the Industrial Revolution took off in Britain, rather than anywhere else, at the end of the 18th century because of the unique influence of the British population's habit for drinking tea.

While many other countries shared with Britain the same levels of technology and skills, it was the Britons' affection for the drink that tipped the balance in providing a steadily increasing and healthy population. For the vigorous increase in activity associated with industrialisation, it was essential to gather people together in towns and cities in proportions quite unlike anything seen before. In past history, when populations conglomerated, they usually succumbed to the spread of disease.

Curiously, in Britain there were steady reductions in child mortality and in common city diseases, especially the water-borne infection, dysentery. Professor Alan Macfarlane discovered a remarkable association between these trends and the increase in tea-drinking. His theory was founded on the fact that tea was drunk with boiled water, which killed off disease-carrying bacteria. Tea also possesses, in tannin, an antiseptic agent which made mothers' breast milk the healthiest it had ever been.

No other nation drank tea on the same scale as the British. This, according to Macfarlane, was the key to why the Industrial Revolution was born here instead of somewhere else.

The present line of the British royal family would not be ruling today had it not been for the strangest twist of fate that saw the most fecund of all Britain's queens fail to produce a single heir – despite giving birth 19 times.

Anne, last of the Stuart line, who became queen in 1702, had been pregnant every year of her life from her marriage in 1683 until 1700. She suffered 14 stillbirths or miscarriages, and gave birth to two sons and three daughters. Only one survived early childhood. He died aged 11 in 1700.

She died in 1714, her body worn out, aged only 49. With no direct heir, the royal line transferred to the Hanoverians. Her second cousin, George, the Elector of Hanover, became George I, from whom our present monarchs are directly descended.

Queen Victoria's rule could have been rendered entirely invalid had the Sub-Dean of Westminster not been paying attention at her coronation in 1838. Towards the end, the Bishop of Bath and Wells, who was presiding at this point, turned over two pages of the order of service by mistake, missing out important parts of the ceremony. The Queen had left Westminster Abbey before the Sub-Dean pointed out the error. She had to be brought back to finish the service properly.

Robert Clive, founder of Britain's empire in India, and one of history's most dynamic military and political leaders, tried to shoot himself in 1744 when he was just 19 – weeks after his arrival in India – because of his debts, but he failed to do so when his pistol misfired twice. He is reported to have announced, 'It appears I am destined for something. I will live.'

He rose to become commander of the East India Company's army, later won the key battle of Plassey which brought large swathes of India under British control, frustrating French ambitions for an Indian empire and establishing the foundations for the British Raj.

He ended up as Governor of Bengal. He also amassed a personal fortune estimated at £4.5 billion in present-day values – all in a career, excluding breaks back in England, of a little under 12 years. He retired at 42, and was dead by 49.

Several hundred Parisians were massacred during a military coup led by Louis-Napoleon Bonaparte in 1851 because the general leading the gendarmerie happened to have a bad cold. The massacre ensured that the coup succeeded and a year later France had another Emperor Napoleon – and all because of that cold.

The nephew of the original Bonaparte, Louis-Napoleon, had got himself elected as President of France in 1848 after the overthrow of the French monarchy. But his dynastic genes were as strong as his uncle's. As he neared the end of his term of office, he engineered a coup in December 1851 to take dictatorial powers. He had brought back from the Foreign Legion in Africa a favourite general, Jacques Leroy de Saint Arnaud, to lead the troops in securing Paris.

The change of weather from the heat of Algeria to a European winter gave Arnaud a terrible cold. As he led his forces to confront a mob resisting the coup he is said to have had a coughing fit. As it ended, he cursed '*Ma sacrée toux*' ('My damned cough!'). The head of the Guard misheard it as '*Massacrez tous*' ('Massacre them all') and launched an assault on the crowd. Up to 800 people are believed to have been killed. It was the pivotal moment in turning the tide of the coup, and paved the way for Napoleon's seizure of power, and eventual elevation to Emperor as Napoleon III. And it all stemmed from Saint Arnaud's misheard curse.

Had a Swiss businessman obtained more efficient customer service from the same Napoleon's bureaucracy, the world might never have had the Red Cross. The idea for the organisation began after another Napoleonic massacre, this time at the Battle of Solferino in June 1859 as the Emperor waged a war of territorial expansion against Austrian control of the minor states of northern Italy. It was an entirely fortuitous coincidence that Jean Henri Dunant was heading for Solferino too, to seek the Emperor's personal help in agreeing concession details for his company. He had spent fruitless months trying to sort out matters with civil servants in Paris.

Dunant arrived in the evening of the day of battle, and witnessed the horrors of the aftermath of 'modern' war. Some 30,000 soldiers were dead or wounded, and there was a complete absence of any medical facilities to aid them.

Appalled, Dunant organised the townspeople to prepare temporary hospitals and with his own money bought medicines. He stressed a neutral attitude of helping both sides without favouritism, which was to become the hallmark of the organisation he was to found when he returned to his home in Geneva.

The horrors had scarred him so much that he wrote up his experiences, published the account in 1862 from his own pocket, and campaigned internationally. He convened the first meeting of an International Committee of the Red Cross in February 1863 in Geneva, which would become the headquarters of the worldwide effort to reduce suffering from war. The following year, the Red Cross produced the first Geneva Convention on the treatment of the wounded in war. Dunant chose the organisation's name and symbol by simply reversing the colours of his own national flag.

He devoted the rest of his life to the cause and, in 1901, nine years before his death, was awarded the inaugural Nobel Peace Prize.

One of the biggest ecological disasters of all time came about because an emigrating hunter missed his pastime. Thomas Austin, a settler in Victoria, Australia, introduced 24 rabbits on to his Winchelsea estate near Melbourne in 1859, with devastating results.

With no natural predators, they had multiplied within 10 years to the extent that it was claimed that upwards of two million could be caught annually without any impact on their numbers. It was the fastest spread of any mammal in recorded history.

By 1950, there were an estimated 600 million rabbits plaguing the countryside. They were reduced to a mere 100 million by an eradication programme through the deliberate release of myxomatosis, but immunity soon developed and numbers are now thought to have risen again to over 300 million.

The impact on the Australian ecology has been devastating. An eighth of all mammalian species on the continent is now extinct, with rabbits being the prime cause. The Australian government currently estimates that the damage to crops and production each year is in the order of $600 million.

An equally bizarre and costly ecological legacy from a gesture of small intentions is the presence in North America today of the common starling. It is not a species natural to the continent, and is regarded by Americans as a nuisance bird. It arrived by virtue of an eccentric 19th century Shakespeare obsessive who gave himself the mission to introduce into America every bird mentioned in Shakespeare's plays.

Eugene Scheifflin, a wealthy drug manufacturer, released just 100 starlings in New York's Central Park in the early 1890s. Within 50 years they had spread across the entire United States. They are now thought to number at least 200 million. Capable of eating one to two times their own weight every day, they are regarded by grain farmers as scavengers, and ornithologists have blamed them for pushing some native species, such as the bluebird and woodpecker, close to extinction. Nationwide, the US Wildlife Service kills a million a year in a losing battle to control their spread. They cause nearly $1 billion of damage to agriculture crops every year.

Ironically, throughout all of the Bard's plays, the starling is mentioned on just one single, solitary occasion (in *Henry IV, Pt I*).

America's purchase of Alaska from Russia in 1867 turned out to be one of the best bargains ever transacted for the United States. At under two cents an acre, the vast land has since yielded billions of dollars worth of treasure, through precious minerals and oil.

But at first, the deal was ridiculed by American politicians and Congress nearly did not agree to provide the funds required. It also proved a complete misfire in regard to the aim America actually had as the reason for the purchase.

Negotiated literally overnight on 29/30 March, the US Secretary of State William Seward saw the main value of the transaction as making it easier to annex Western Canada, a long-held American objective. Anti-British feeling after the ending of the Civil War two years earlier, in which Britain had been sympathetic to the rebellious Confederacy, had begun to spur expansionist sentiment against Britain's presence in Canada.

In fact, the Alaska purchase worked in the opposite direction. It pushed the western provinces even more strongly down the path towards joining the Federation, which was about to be established by the eastern provinces that year. Within four years, British Columbia, the most vulnerable colony, had actually become part of a Federal Canada.

For Russia, the motivation was even less profound. Tsar Alexander II's government was desperately short of money. Part of the reason had been an expensive naval expedition the Russian admiralty had laid on during the American Civil War to send a fleet of ships to visit New York and San Francisco as a goodwill gesture and a tacit warning to Britain against its support for the Confederacy.

One story has it that of the $7.2 million the United States paid for Alaska, $5.8 million (80 per cent) was to reimburse the Russians for the costs of the tour. Had the Russians not wanted to cock a snook at Britain, they might have been able to afford to keep Alaska long enough for its true worth to emerge and, a century later, the Cold War could have taken on a completely different dimension.

The Eiffel Tower in Paris was originally built for the 1889 Universal Exposition held to mark the centenary of the French Revolution. The city authorities granted the builders of the tower a licence to occupy the site for just 20 years, after which the tower would be demolished. (One of the rules of the original competition was that the resulting tower could be easily taken down.)

When 1909 came, the city was still intent on demolition. The presence of a single radio antenna at the summit saved the tower. The city was persuaded by French telegraph officials and the army that the tower was serving as a useful transmitting beacon. It was on those grounds that the Eiffel Tower was allowed to remain.

The Panama Canal would have been built in Nicaragua had it not been for a lobbyist's use of a postage stamp.

After the success of its Suez Canal, France had, as far back as 1878, purchased the rights to build a canal across Panama, but had failed for years to put together the necessary finances. In 1902, the most fervent advocate, engineer Philippe Jean Bunau-Varilla, went to the United States to lobby for American interest in backing the project. He discovered that a Bill was before the Senate proposing a canal further north, across Nicaragua, taking advantage of its huge lake which could be used for nearly half the 140 miles required.

The prospect severely threatened French interests. Bunau-Varilla countered by pointing to the array of volcanoes in

Nicaragua, which by implication threatened the viability of the canal there. The US State Department, the 'experts', suggested that they never erupted. The majority opinion in the Senate accepted this and appeared to be heading inexorably in favour of endorsing the Nicaraguan route.

Bunau-Varilla then pulled off his masterstroke. He was aware that a current Nicaraguan five-pesos stamp proudly portrayed an image of one of the country's small volcanoes in full eruption.

He wrote a letter to every senator emblazoned with one of the stamps, asking whether American taxpayers would be happy to risk their investment to the volcanoes. The letters arrived on senators' desks three days before the crucial vote. When it was taken, the Senate decided in favour of Panama by 42–34. And so it was to be.

*

The headquarters of the United Nations would have been in Philadelphia, not New York, had philanthropist tycoon John D. Rockefeller Jnr not gifted $8.5 million (worth close to $250 million in modern values) for the purchase of derelict land along the East River for the purpose. But his motivation was not entirely altruistic. Had a rival idea for using the land not been viewed as a clear threat to his own business empire, he might not have bailed out the new international organisation with his incredible generosity.

Philadelphia was so confident of its success – it had identified a huge area of condemned land near the University of Pennsylvania – that the City Council had set up planning hearings for a week before the UN was due to decide the issue in December 1946. The two other potential cities, San Francisco and Boston, had dropped by the wayside.

Rockefeller was well aware that a real estate planner, William Zeckendorf, had big ideas for the East River area. 'X-City' was to be a vast modern development, a 'city within a city', of four 40-storey office blocks at one end, three 30-storey apartment towers housing

7,500 families at the other, and, in the middle, two 57-storey curved slabs containing a hotel, convention centre, opera and concert halls. There would also be a heliport and yacht marina on the river front.

It was a blatant attempt to rival and surpass Rockefeller's own Rockefeller Center across town. Aware that his own building was only 60 per cent occupied, X-City represented an acute threat to the Rockefeller organisation's future. So Rockefeller did what tycoons can do. He made Zeckendorf an offer he could not refuse to buy him out and gifted the site to the UN. It was announced the day the UN's deadline was up. The UN breathed a sigh of relief. Whether it was as big as Rockefeller's, no one will ever know.

Rockefeller even used Zeckendorf's plans to suggest the layout of the UN, pencilling in 'General Assembly' over the planned opera hall and 'Security', 'Economic & Social', and 'Trusteeship' over the other auditoriums for the councils that would form part of the UN system.

A letter that surfaced in 2000, written by the second-in-command of Captain Scott's ill-fated Antarctic expedition in 1912, added an intriguing twist to the reasons for Scott's disastrous end.

Lt Edward Evans, who led a support group for part of the outward leg to the Pole before turning back, deplored Scott's decision to insist on dragging 150lb of scientific finds and geological records even when the party was short of provisions and clearly in life-threatening trouble. 'We dumped ours at the first check. I must say I considered the safety of my party before the value of the records…Apparently, Scott did not….he ought to have left it, pushed on and recovered the specimens and records [later].'

During Scott's return, one man fell to his death and Captain Oates famously walked out in a blizzard to die. Scott and the remaining two perished in their tent. After an 800-mile trek dragging their heavy sleds, they were only 11 miles from the safety of a large food store.

Adolf Hitler's father was born Alois Schicklgruber. Alois was the illegitimate offspring of Maria Schicklgruber, an unmarried peasant woman from the village of Strones in the Waldviertal, a backward part of northern Austria, and an unknown father. Alois went under his mother's surname for the first five years of his life and lived in the single-parent household until, for reasons that remain unknown, one Johann Georg Heidler married Maria.

No one knows who Alois's true father was. The fact that Alois continued to keep the name Schicklgruber for the next 35 years strongly suggests that it wasn't Johann. He was still a Schicklgruber when Johann died 15 years after becoming his stepfather.

He might have remained a Schicklgruber all his life – and hence given birth to Adolf Schicklgruber, not Adolf Hitler – had the self-interest of Alois and a step-uncle not combined.

By the time Alois was 40, and working his way into a respectable civil service career, he had an interest in legitimising himself. Johann's brother also faced a problem – the extinction of the Heidler family name because he had three daughters and no sons. He wrote a will promising Alois money if he agreed to officially change his name.

Alois did so and, changing the spelling, became Alois Hitler.

What is the historical significance of this small change? Can anyone imagine that someone tagged Adolf Schicklgruber would have been able to carve as successful a political career as Adolf Hitler did? *Heil Schicklgruber?*

16

Edmund Hillary and the Sherpa, Tenzing Norgay, were not the intended conquerors of Mount Everest in 1953. They were the back-up pair. Before their successful climb, expedition leader Colonel John Hunt sent up his first team, comprising Tom Bourdillon and Charles Evans, Hunt's deputy.

Bourdillon was a fitting choice as he had been mainly responsible for the design of the breathing equipment that had enabled them to survive this far. But misfortune was to strike an ironic blow. Less than 300 feet from the summit, his partner, Evans, encountered a problem with his breathing gear. The pair realised they would not make it to the top and returned down to the camp.

Three days later, on 29 May, it was the number two pair who were standing on the summit, and whose names would for ever be remembered by history. Who now has even heard of Bourdillon or Evans?

An oversight in preparation meant that there is no photograph of Hillary on the summit of Everest. The single famous shot is of Tenzing. Asked to explain the historic omission, Hillary said, 'As far as I knew, Tenzing had never taken a photograph before and the summit of Everest was hardly the place to show him how.'

The strangely named Alaskan city of Nome is said to derive its name from a mapmaker's mistake. According to the city's legend, around the 1850s a navigator sailing up the Bering Sea mapping the area miscopied an older map which had annotated the as yet unnamed place as '? Name.' The navigator misread this as 'C. Nome' for Cape Nome, and the promontory near the present city was thus christened.

The settlement that sprung up there in 1898, as a result of a gold rush, was forced by the US Post Office to adopt the tag of the nearby Cape. The town's original wish to name itself Anvil City was refused as it was too close to another settlement in the Yukon.

Greenland got its oddly inappropriate name because its attributes were deliberately misrepresented by its promoter to attract unsuspecting settlers.

The first explorer to land there, the Norwegian Eric the Red in 982, found the place, not surprisingly, uninhabited. Although some portions on the coast were actually lushly verdant, at least enough to sustain a population, he chose to mask the general barrenness of the place when he returned home and began agitating for emigration to colonise the huge island.

Seven hundred people ventured out on the first journey there three years later. Only 14 of the 25 ships that started actually made it due to the atrocious sea conditions. Again, perhaps not surprisingly then, once they had got there, few had the stomach to turn around and leave.

2

Politics – Fates and Fortunes

The British Cabinet system of government – elected ministers led by a prime minister meeting separately from the monarch's presence – became a regular practice after 1717 when the German-born King George I stopped attending meetings of his ministers. Legend has it that this was due to him not understanding English. This is only partially true: Cabinet meetings had actually been held in French, which he could speak, for the three years after his accession in 1714. But they were not successful and led to many misunderstandings. Another motive for stopping was that it was difficult for George to deny the right of his son, the Prince of Wales, to preside as regent in the king's absence, and, as he detested his son, he wanted to avoid his involvement. Whichever of these motives was the predominant one, Britain's invention of Cabinet government originated for these distinctly unorthodox and unplanned reasons.

The glue that holds the British decision-making process together was the invention of the concept of 'collective responsibility' for Cabinets – the practice that once a decision has been made in Cabinet, all ministers publicly support it (even if they disagreed in the original arguments). This, too, originated from the idiosyncrasies of a king, this time George III in the mid-18th century.

19

He had the habit of conducting business with ministers in a private room called the Closet, and to meet with them only one at a time. This caused problems by threatening the cohesiveness of governments as the king would often use the one-on-one meetings to his advantage by swaying individual ministers against any policy he objected to. So ministers developed the practice of agreeing in advance what they would say and they also agreed to stick to the identical story as they each had their audiences with the king.

The famous home of British prime ministers since 1735, No. 10 Downing Street, only became the official residence because its first occupant suspected it was so badly built it would soon fall down, and he wanted the public purse to bear the expense.

Robert Walpole, our first recognised prime minister, was offered the house in 1732 as a personal gift by the Crown, but the sly old wheeler-dealer suspected he would be taking on a liability. He refused to accept the gift because he knew the foundations of Downing Street were built on shifting silt that came up from the Thames just yards away. The house would be a perpetual cause of expense to him if he owned it himself. So he sneakily professed to George II a degree of humility that forbade him to accept such ostentatious largesse personally, but he gladly accepted it in his official capacity as First Lord of the Treasury, the early title of the prime minister. He took up residence on 22 September and stayed there until his demise seven years later.

The tradition nearly stopped then, with no prime minister residing at No. 10 for over two decades until George Grenville resumed the practice when he took office in 1763. From then on, prime ministers, with one or two exceptions, have been there ever since – and at the public's expense.

Walpole was probably right in his judgement about the solidity of the buildings in Downing Street. In the early 1960s, a major refurbishment programme effectively had to rebuild No. 10. The contractor was quoted as saying, 'Sir George Downing was the greatest jerry-builder of his time…worse than the jerry-builders of today.'

The standards and public expectations of politicians have changed markedly down the years, not least due to the growing importance of the media as an essential tool of modern political life. Today, the smallest foible or indiscretion can be a death sentence to a political career, or at the very least an awkward situation to resolve through deft PR management.

Ever-changing social mores throw up some intriguing historical questions. Many of our past political heroes excelled in their own times with extraordinary panache – but would they have done so today, if they had lived under the spotlight politicians now endure? The accident of timing allowed them to be successes. Would any of these have managed to survive in a modern tabloid world?

Robert Walpole, the inaugural British PM, spent three months locked up in the Tower of London on corruption charges in 1712 when Secretary at War. It did not stop him being appointed Chancellor of the Exchequer three years later on his path to the top.

William Pitt, who became prime minister at the age of 24 in 1783 and remained in office for the next 17 years, was addicted to a bottle of port a day (by the end of his short life it was up to three) and was frequently drunk when in the House of Commons. He famously once left his seat during a debate to vomit behind the Speaker's chair, and returned to make a superb prime ministerial speech.

His father, **Pitt the Elder**, had been prime minister a generation before (1766-68). He was a manic-depressive, had had a mental breakdown in 1751 while a Cabinet minister (Paymaster General) and had withdrawn from public office for three years. While serving in the highest office, clear signs of mental instability were evident. He spent most of his prime ministership sequestered away in a small room in his house at Hampstead, trying to avoid his ministers and the pressures of governing. During his time, his Chancellor was doing his own thing, unwisely levying the taxes on the North American colonies that would eventually ignite the War of Independence.

Earl Grey, who served from 1830 to 1834 and who introduced the Great Reform Act of 1832 that revolutionised electoral representation, had sat in parliament for 44 years before he reached the top and yet had just 15 months of ministerial experience. On his appointment, he named 20 of his relations to jobs in government.

Lord Melbourne, favourite and fatherly mentor to the young Queen Victoria, and prime minister for six years, mainly in the late 1830s, was a philanderer with the unique record for prime ministers of having been cited in two court actions brought by angry husbands for seducing their wives. He was also a flagellant with an unhealthy sexual interest in whipping, particularly children, and sending pictures cut from erotic French books to his mistress. Melbourne also developed the unfortunate habit of falling asleep at the wrong moments, on one occasion doing so three times during an audience with the Queen.

Lord Palmerston was granted his first seat in parliament in 1807, by the owner of a 'rotten borough' (where the landlord controlled the small number of voters) in the Isle of Wight, on the condition that he never set foot in the constituency. The owner did not want him to generate a local following. Palmerston was also a notorious womaniser, described by one contemporary diarist as 'always enterprising and audacious with women', even into his late years (he first became prime minister in 1855 at the age of 71 and died in office two days short of his 81st birthday). He was accused of adultery when he was 78, which appeared merely to enhance his popularity. He is supposed to have fathered an illegitimate child when nearly 80. Early in his career, when he applied to join a select London club, it was strongly rumoured that of the seven lady patronesses on whom the final decision rested, at least three were his lovers. He even once tried to seduce a royal lady-in-waiting at Windsor Castle while a guest of the Queen.

Benjamin Disraeli was bankrupted at 21 by his participation in a fraudulent mining company share scandal during a heady stock market boom in the mid-1820s. Working as a lawyer's clerk, his literary talent was used to puff up a prospectus for a fictitious Mexican mining project. While it is not likely he knew the full extent of the fraud, such questionable judgement could well have put a stop to a career in public office in later times. He ran his first election campaign desperately trying to keep out of public sight because of the creditors pursuing him.

William Gladstone, stalwart of Victorian probity, when both chancellor and prime minister made midnight sojourns around the seedier haunts of London's Piccadilly and Soho on a high-minded mission to save prostitutes. He would invite them home to meet his wife, give them support money, arrange for them to get food and shelter, and for some of them to have a holiday out of the city by the seaside. He pursued this activity across 30 years, between the late 1840s and the 1880s, starting with his co-founding in 1848 of the Church Penitentiary Association for the Reclamation of Fallen Women. His activities became widely known in Westminster political circles. When one man who followed him in 1853 tried to blackmail him, Gladstone simply marched him to a police station and pressed charges. When the story reached the newspapers, editors to a man protected him. Most historians express bemusement at the practice but tend towards accepting the innocent explanation, but there is no doubt that his solitary walks in the early hours would never have been as easily defended had he lived a century later.

At the time of the outbreak of the First World War in 1914, **Sir Edward Grey**, foreign secretary since 1905, had never even visited Europe, apart from a non-stop journey through the continent to India and a brief state visit to Paris.

Herbert Asquith, prime minister for eight years until halfway through the First World War, became so besotted with his daughter's best friend, 25-year-old Venetia Stanley, that between 1912 and 1915 he spent many Cabinet meetings writing love letters to her. He was in his early 60s, at the time. In the first three months of 1915, he wrote to her 151 times. There was also concern about his drinking. During the committee stage of the landmark Parliament Bill in 1911, Asquith was slumped in his prime ministerial position on the front bench in the House of Commons, too drunk to speak.

David Lloyd George, who followed Asquith and was perhaps one of Britain's greatest prime ministers, in war and in peace, and probably the last to have been able to 'get away with it', was nicknamed 'The Goat' because of his womanising antics. His secretary had become his mistress four years before he became prime minister in 1916, and remained so until his wife died in 1941. While prime minister, Lloyd George also survived his questionable practice of selling honours for money, and, in 1912 when Chancellor of the Exchequer, a share scandal in which he appears to have benefited from inside knowledge of government contracts.

Would any of these have survived the modern day inquisition by television's political pundits or the exposés by the scandal-seeking press?

For over four years after November 1892, Winston Churchill was the heir apparent to the Dukedom of Marlborough following the death of the 8th Duke and the succession of Churchill's cousin, Charles. It was to be 1897 before Charles and his wife produced a son, and a direct heir. Had Charles died before producing an heir, Churchill would have been bound to take the title and his political career would have been very different to the one he is now remembered for.

In an era long before the acceptability of renouncing titles for political expediency, Churchill would have been banished to the House of Lords amid a period of social transformation that was to see within a generation the unelected House disappear from any governing influence of the country.

Churchill was just 18 in 1892, and still studying for a military cadetship. Any thought of a leading career in British politics would have been over before it had even germinated.

Benjamin Disraeli, one of the most flamboyant and successful 19th-century prime ministers, came within a stroke of a fatal challenge to his integrity early on in his parliamentary life that could have stopped his career dead in its tracks.

Initially a supporter of Prime Minister Sir Robert Peel when he was elected in 1837 at the age of 32, by the next election in 1841 he had established himself as the darling of the party for his wit and precociousness and he confidently expected to be included in Peel's Cabinet. He was not. Mortified, he wrote a letter appealing for a position, but to no avail.

The humiliation pushed him into a personal vendetta against Peel and as an economic crisis brewed in the following years over the price of bread and the Corn Laws, which kept prices high, Disraeli launched a campaign of guerrilla attacks on his own leader.

It came to a head in 1846 when Peel had to repeal the Corn Laws. Disraeli spoke bitingly against him in the House of Commons debate. Peel's riposte was to question why, if Disraeli was so opposed to him, he had asked for a ministerial job under his leadership. Here Disraeli came within an ace of a public disgrace that would have curtailed his meteoric rise.

Disraeli, caught by surprise, lied by denying to the House that he had ever written asking for a job. He took a risk that Peel had not kept the letter. Unknown to him, Peel had kept it and some sources suggest he even had it on him that evening but could not find it amongst his papers in time. Another suggests that Peel's own hyper-sense of honour made him feel it would be unfair to read out a personal communication.

Had he produced it, Disraeli's chances of future glory would have been in tatters. As it was, Peel resigned after the Corn Laws debacle, the Conservative Party split for a generation and when it came together again in the late 1860s, it was Disraeli who was at the helm. He remained Conservative leader until his death in 1881.

One of the most far-reaching political reforms of the 20th century in Britain – the extension of the vote to all adult women – came about entirely by accident through a single incautious and unplanned remark by the Conservative Home Secretary in the House of Commons during a dull Friday afternoon debate on the subject.

William Joynson-Hicks, one of the most unorthodox home secretaries there has ever been, was speaking for the Government on 20 February 1925, opposing a private member's Bill to give women the vote at 21. (Since 1918, only women aged 30 and over had had the vote.) Startlingly, when interrupted by Lady Astor, an ardent supporter of the reform, he responded with a firm commitment to introduce the measure at the next election.

He had no Cabinet authority to make the pledge, had not discussed it with colleagues and, worse, employed a quotation by the Prime Minister Stanley Baldwin in support, making it almost impossible to backtrack. There is no evidence either that he had planned to say what he did.

Having made the pledge, and used the Prime Minister's name, the Cabinet felt obliged to see it through. The law was changed in 1928 and the following year's General Election was the first universal suffrage election in Britain's history.

Without his off-the-cuff remark, there is little reason to think that the tranquillity-seeking Baldwin, one of the most cautious of all Conservative premiers, would have found it a government priority to grant the 'flapper' vote. Winston Churchill was to write of the episode several years later, 'Never was so great a change in our electorate achieved so incontinently. For good or ill, [Joynson-Hicks] should always be remembered for that.'

'Jix', as he was known, did not stand again for election, was elevated to the House of Lords as Lord Brentford and died three years later. He never explained what had possessed him to be so forward that Friday afternoon.

A fleeting encounter with a journalist cost Hugh Dalton, Labour Chancellor of the Exchequer and one of the leading politicians of his generation, his post in November 1947 and, it turned out, his career. The incident was one of the most bizarre in modern British politics, abounding with twists of misfortune.

As Dalton made his way through the Palace of Westminster to the Commons to deliver the Budget speech, he bumped into John Carvel, political correspondent of the London evening paper, the *Star*. The newsman tried his arm and asked what was in the Budget. He could hardly have expected to be told as Budget decisions were naturally the closest of secrets until they had been announced publicly in parliament.

Dalton assumed that Carvel was likewise on the way to the press gallery to listen to the Budget. In a succinct summary of his plans, he told Carvel, 'No more on tobacco; a penny on beer; something on dogs and [football] pools but not on horses; increase in purchase tax, but only on articles now taxable; profits tax doubled.'

Instead of proceeding to the House, Carvel telephoned his editor and editions of the *Star* were on sale 20 minutes before Dalton reached that part of his speech. Although there was no practical damage done, Dalton tendered his resignation the next day. He was brought back to the Cabinet the following year, but he never regained his former standing.

Other factors combined to create the disaster. That he ran into the journalist in the first place was highly unlucky. The Commons were still using the House of Lords chamber while their own bomb-damaged home was under repair. Had that not been so, Dalton would not have entered through the route that exposed him to the casual presence of journalists. Had his deputy, Douglas Jay, who would have been alongside him at the fateful moment, not been sent off to ensure that there was water at the despatch box for the speech, he might well have been able to discourage Dalton from stopping to chat.

And it later turned out that Carvel himself had not planned the ambush. He was dared by a colleague on the spur of the moment.

A would-be minister, who has remained unidentified, ruined his career when he mishandled a meeting with Prime Minister Clement Attlee, who was offering him a senior post in the Cabinet. Attlee was one of the most taciturn leaders ever. As the aspirant went into fawning mode expressing how inadequate he felt he was for such an important position, Attlee cut him short with an 'all right then' and withdrew the job offer.

Harold Wilson and Tony Blair, two of Labour's most influential prime ministers in Britain, were both accidental leaders. They achieved elevation unexpectedly after the early deaths of leaders who were cast for lengthy tenures at the top. Wilson succeeded after the sudden death in January 1963 of Hugh Gaitskell from a rare autoimmune disease at the early age of 56. Blair succeeded in July 1994 following the sudden death from a heart attack of John Smith, aged just 55. Smith had been party leader for less than two years.

Wilson would go on to be prime minister for nearly eight years in all, and Blair for just over ten.

The rescheduling of BBC's most popular television sitcom may have settled the outcome of the 1964 General

Election. With opinion polls showing the leading parties neck and neck, Labour's Harold Wilson, who was trying to oust the Conservatives after 13 years in office, was deeply worried by the fact that *Steptoe and Son* was due to be shown at 8 o'clock on election night, just an hour before the polls closed. He felt this would adversely affect Labour's turnout as the majority of the show's audience was likely to be their supporters. He protested to the Corporation's Director-General, Sir Hugh Greene, who eventually agreed to postpone the show until nine. Wilson thanked Greene saying, 'That will be worth a dozen or more seats to me.' Labour won by just four. Greene later said that he had always wondered 'whether I should have a bad conscience.'

Conservative Prime Minister of Britain Harold Macmillan would have fought the 1964 General Election against Labour new boy Harold Wilson had he not falsely believed he had cancer.

He had decided in the autumn of 1963 to retire in early 1964 and not contest the election, but on 7 October he changed his mind and decided he would lead the government into the election after all. The next day, however, he was unexpectedly hospitalised for surgery on his prostate, which was initially diagnosed as cancerous. He wrote out a resignation statement to be read at the party conference. One account has suggested that the conference chairman, Lord Home, who (perhaps not so) coincidentally would succeed Macmillan as prime minister, rushed the statement to the conference and read it out before Macmillan could change his mind again. It later turned out that he did not have cancer. He made a respectable recovery and did not die until 1986 at the ripe old age of 92.

It was left for the (de-titled) Alec Douglas-Home, famously chastised by Wilson as 'the 14th Earl of Home' (the title he had disclaimed) to fight against the youthful Labour leader. Wilson, as we have seen, squeaked home by a narrow majority of four.

In light of the startling social cleavage presented by the two adversaries, it is an intriguing thought whether in such a tight battle the more experienced and in touch Macmillan might just have held the Conservatives in office had he been at the helm.

Prime Minister Jim Callaghan's decision in September 1978 not to call a General Election that autumn but to continue into a fifth and final year of office turned out to be a disastrous decision that, eight months later, ushered in his Conservative opponent, Margaret Thatcher, and ejected the Labour Party from government for nearly a generation.

The decision astonished every political observer as the weeks before had built up an almost unstoppable momentum for calling an election. The Government was struggling to keep a parliamentary majority, and a pact with the small Liberal Party had just ended. The Government was, however, only 2 per cent behind the Conservatives in the most recent opinion polls.

Even as Callaghan broadcast to the nation on the evening of 7 September, everyone expected it to be because he was going to announce the date for an October election. Instead, he baulked. He would not, he told the expectant electorate, 'seek your votes because there is some blue sky overhead today.'

He ploughed on. He encountered the 'Winter of Discontent', a series of strikes by public sector workers that left rubbish uncollected in the streets and bodies unburied in morgues. His government was eventually defeated – by one vote – in a confidence debate in March 1979, and in May, Mrs Thatcher inflicted the heaviest defeat on an incumbent government since the war.

Ironically, in the previous October, when the election could have been held, Gallup opinion polls showed the Government enjoying a five-point lead over the Conservatives. They would have won the election handsomely. They maintained the lead until December when the strikes began to bite, and never recovered.

Had Labour won in 1978, and with the next election not then

due until 1983, it becomes an intriguing question whether Mrs Thatcher would have lasted as Conservative leader. She would have been at the party's helm in Opposition for seven years. No Conservative leader – before or since – has spent so long as leader without having brought the party a place in government.

Harold Wilson became famous for always having his pipe with him. He started the practice entirely as a television prop. During his first television broadcast after becoming leader, his trusted adviser, Marcia Williams, warned him that his habit of raising his fist to emphasise a point looked threatening to the viewer. They decided that he should carry his pipe in one of his hands to stop himself. It worked, and became a fixture of his image. He actually preferred large cigars and would usually smoke one after lunch. It was a sight he carefully kept from the screen in favour of the classless pipe.

Williams encouraged him in another habit too. He tended to rest his left hand on his face during interviews. She told him to carry on as it showed off his wedding ring. 'You had this comfortable picture of the dependable young family man – it gave the image of reassurance,' Williams confided, according to Michael Cockerell's 'Live from No. 10', his chronicle of early political television.

Karl Marx's *Das Kapital*, which lays out the principles of Communism, was so convolutedly written that the official censor allowed it for translation into Russian on the grounds that it was a 'difficult and hardly comprehensible' work that 'few would read and still fewer understand. It is unlikely to find many readers among the general public.'

The film of John Steinbeck's biting, Depression-era

31

novel, ***The Grapes of Wrath***, was passed by the Soviet censors because it portrayed an unattractive picture of life for the working classes in the capitalist United States. It was later banned when the authorities discovered that audiences were enormously impressed by the fact that the poor, itinerant farming family of the story, meant to represent America's dispossessed, owned their own car.

Ignorance also worked in the opposite direction. During the notorious McCarthy anti-Communist witch-hunt in the United States in the 1950s, popular hysteria could be whipped up with amazing ease. To illustrate the public's dangerous suspension of common sense, William Evjue, editor of the *Capital Times*, a newspaper in McCarthy's home state of Wisconsin, who had launched a campaign to expose McCarthyism, had a reporter stand on a street corner in the state capital, Madison, asking passers-by to sign a petition. It was in fact the American Declaration of Independence. Of 112 people approached to sign it, 111 thought it subversive and refused.

It is one of the ironies of Marx's life that had he not forged his close friendship with Friedrich Engels, the wealthy son of a cotton factory capitalist who continually sent him money to keep the family out of destitution, Marx would never have been able to support himself, and might literally have starved to death.

The two key leaders of the 1917 Bolshevik revolution in Russia, Lenin and Trotsky, both found their way into the country through foreign help, one deliberate and one accidental. Without these fortuitous actions, neither would have played the central roles they did which were crucial to the eventual Communist success.

In February 1917, at the height of the First World War, the

smaller Menshevik faction had overthrown the Tsar in the first of the two revolutions that year. Lenin, the leader of the larger Bolsheviks, was in exile in Switzerland. The Germans calculated that Lenin's presence back in St Petersburg could add to the general disruption and reduce Russia's ability to carry on the war against them. They arranged for Lenin to be transported by sealed train across German territory, in Churchill's celebrated words, 'like a plague bacillus into Russia.' Lenin would spearhead the opposition to the Menshevik regime, culminating in the October Revolution and the ushering in of 75 years of the Soviet Union.

MI5 documents, only released in 2001, revealed that Lenin's right-hand man, Leon Trotsky, founder of the Red Army, was under surveillance by the agency after the outbreak of the February Revolution. He was in exile in New York and trying to return to Russia to challenge the new government. MI5 tracked him as he left America on a ship bound for St Petersburg and in March arrested him in Halifax, Nova Scotia.

He would have remained there, out of touch with the Communists' struggle, had it not been for the intervention of MI5's sister agency, MI6, the overseas intelligence service. MI6 believed that the information about Trotsky used by MI5 had been planted by an agent provocateur, and persuaded the Canadian authorities to release him. Within a month of his arrest, Trotsky was back on a ship heading for Russia and his role as leading war maker in the civil war that guaranteed the Bolsheviks' victory.

Lenin miraculously survived an assassination attempt in 1918, less than a year after the launch of the Russian revolution. The country was embroiled in civil war, the outcome of which was far from clear. His death then might have led to any number of eventualities for Russia.

He was leaving a Moscow factory, where he had given a speech on 30 August, when a woman, Fanya Kaplan, apparently complaining about food shortages, fired three shots that hit Lenin in the neck, shoulder and chest. Remarkably, he lived.

Had he died, in the midst of war, he would probably have been succeeded by his powerful Red Army head, Leon Trotsky, averting the catastrophe that was to follow under Stalin. He lived, though, for another five years, by which time a period of peace had reduced Trotsky's significance and allowed Stalin to build a power base.

When Lenin eventually died in January 1924, Stalin was the more effective in manoeuvring himself into pole position.

How close Lenin came to dying that day only emerged later. It was four years before he was strong enough to undergo surgery. When doctors recovered the bullets, one was found to be a dum-dum bullet designed to explode on impact. It had failed to do so. Even more strange, it was discovered that the casing had been smeared with curare, a deadly poison. Quite how Lenin survived remains an astonishing mystery.

As a 16-year-old, all Adolf Hitler dreamed of wanting to do with his life was to become an artist or an architect. He applied to the Academy of Fine Arts in Vienna twice but the examiners rejected him because of the poor quality of his test drawings. The Academy's Dean thought he showed a talent for architecture, but the architectural school refused to relax its rule requiring a high school diploma, which Hitler did not possess.

On such decisions the fate of generations would turn.

Hitler's family doctor was so worried about the disturbed state and frequent nightmares of the six-year-old Adolf that he recommended to his mother that the boy should be sent for treatment to a children's mental hospital in Vienna. Evidence suggests it was likely to have been the institution run by Sigmund Freud.

It did not happen. Hitler's mother is believed to have rejected the advice since it was likely it would reveal the often brutal treatment Hitler received at his stern father's hands.

Who knows what effect the analysis might have had on the young personality?

When Hitler became Chancellor of Germany in January 1933, he was the fourth to hold the office in just nine months. His appointment was the result of a complicated power-sharing deal to end a period of political chaos that had seen governments fall after just months, and no fewer than three general elections in two years.

The Nazi Party held only two other seats in the 11-man Cabinet, both minor posts, Interior and a Minister without Portfolio. Hitler had been appointed as a compromise. At the most recent election in November, the Nazis had seen their share of the vote fall for the first time since 1928 and the more moderate leaders had agreed to the appointment, believing that Hitler's power was on the wane and they would be keeping him under their control.

Franz von Papen, a former Chancellor and now Vice Chancellor, was quietly satisfied that the Nazi firebrand had been neutered: 'We have him framed in.' He would learn differently within months.

The United States might have been a monarchy had a German prince made up his mind more quickly. In 1786, as the Constitutional Convention was being planned, a group of senior members of the Continental Congress, Alexander Hamilton, Nathaniel Gortham, the presiding officer of the Congress and James Monroe, who would become a future president, wrote to Prince Henry of Prussia, the younger brother of King Frederick the Great, inviting him to become King of the United States.

If he had accepted promptly, it might have been too awkward later to turn him down when the Convention considered the issue in depth. However, the prince dithered, and then sent a noncommittal reply. By the time the Convention opened the following year, the idea of a monarchy for the United States stood no chance in the staunchly anti-regal gathering.

They were perhaps luckier than they knew. The recommendation had come from Baron Friedrich von Steuben, a Prussian-immigrant hero of the War of Independence who had revolutionised military training for George Washington. He was also a closet homosexual. Unknown to the Americans, Prince Henry was also gay, with a reputation as one of the most debauched homosexuals in Europe.

Medical research published in 2004 claimed that a bout of tuberculosis suffered by George Washington when he was 19 years old may have left him infertile and altered the course of American history.

After leading the Revolutionary Army in the War of Independence, Washington spurned the urgings of some of his colleagues to take up a strong military-style leadership of the new nation, or even become king himself. Many feared that a new republican government run under the untested notion of democracy would be fragile while a monarchy under Washington's benevolent tutelage would be certain to bring stability.

Washington rejected the request to become king (the regal name George I was proposed). His selfless denial of power paved the way for America's republican constitution. The modern research prompts the alluring question whether Washington did so simply because he knew he would never have any children who might one day inherit his title.

Car tycoon Henry Ford might well have become president of the United States in 1924 but for the unexpected, and possibly suspicious, death of his opponent. The incumbent president, Warren Harding, who has been ranked by American historians as among the worst to occupy the office, led a notoriously corrupt administration pockmarked by a series of financial and political scandals.

As the controversies mounted and the 1924 election approached over the horizon, Ford seriously considered running for president. He was at the peak of his popularity as the creator of the Model T, which had given affordable mobility to mass America. An influential opinion poll in the summer of 1923 showed that he would comfortably defeat Harding in an election.

Then, that August, Harding suddenly died. (Some have speculated that he was poisoned by his wife because of his adultery. She refused to allow an autopsy to be held.) He was succeeded by his vice-president, Calvin Coolidge, a shy, restrained and eminently cautious character. Crucially, in the year left before the election, Coolidge's calmness restored respectability to the presidency. The country was wealthy and at peace, the economy stable. In 1924, Coolidge ran on a campaign slogan of 'Keep Cool with Coolidge'. It did. He went on to win an overwhelming victory.

Ford had seen the change of fortune by the end of 1923 and Coolidge's mastery of the political art. He quietly dropped out of the race. If only it had been Harding fighting for his country's vote…

In 1940, a 27-year-old struggling lawyer went into partnership with a group of businessmen in his home town of Whittier, California, to manufacture and sell frozen orange juice. He was appointed company president of Citra-Frost, but within 18 months the enterprise failed – surprisingly, as California was prosperous, had plentiful supplies of oranges, and marketing a convenience product should have had wide appeal.

Had the business worked, the company President might have simply become a successful and wealthy local entrepreneur. As it was, he turned to politics and set his eyes on a different presidency. His name was Richard M. Nixon.

Ronald Reagan, the slayer of the 'Evil Empire', might have been ruined before his political career began had his attempt to join the American Communist Party succeeded. He was rejected because the Communists thought him too dim.

It emerged in a 1999 authorised biography that he had tried to join in 1938 when starting out as a 27-year-old actor in Hollywood. Some of his closest friends were members. One, scriptwriter Howard Fast, revealed that he had felt 'passionate' about it. 'He felt that if it was right for them it was right for him.'

But the Party refused him. 'They thought he was a feather brain…a flake who couldn't be trusted with a political opinion for more than 20 minutes.' As the anti-Communist purges and blacklisting in Hollywood in the 1940s and 1950s destroyed many careers, Reagan's flourished as an actor, then as President of the Screen Actors Guild, the actors' union. And most importantly, his political credentials remained all-American.

If only the Communists had thought more highly of him, he might never been allowed to rise to be their nemesis half a century later.

President-to-be Lyndon Johnson got his break into the big time in 1948 when he won his first Senate race in Texas in a rigged election. He beat his rival, former state governor, Coke Stevenson, by a mere 87 votes out of 988,000.

In the week before voting day, it looked as if he would lose a tight race. The results from a single precinct swung it. When the returns from the tiny border town of Alice came in they showed that 203 people had voted at the last minute, and 202 of them for Johnson. They had all voted in the order in which they were listed in the tax rolls.

Despite a protest from Stevenson, a court upheld the result.

Johnson never looked back. Nearly 30 years later, the election judge in the town admitted that he had rigged the result.

John F. Kennedy's 1960 presidential election victory over Richard Nixon remains one of the closest in America's history. In votes, Kennedy won by just 118,000 in the total of 68 million cast. (He actually won fewer states – 22 to Nixon's 26 – but prevailed because the states he won carried more delegates in the Electoral Convention that finally elects a US President.)

The election was the first to hold televised debates between the candidates. Kennedy is credited as having won the first in Chicago by coming over as fitter, more composed, tanned and altogether more dynamic. Nixon, by contrast, looked haggard, ruffled, nervous – he sweated profusely under the hot lights – and was judged to be less trustworthy. The images stuck, and there is a strong consensus amongst historians of the first truly televised campaign that Nixon's chances were severely dented by the performance.

The reason for Nixon's demeanour was a bang on the knee. Nixon had just come out of hospital where he had spent 12 days on his back after hitting his knee on a car door as he got out of his car during campaigning in North Carolina. He developed an infection which took him out of the contest for nearly a fortnight and, more importantly for the televised debate, drained him of a lot of energy. He had lost weight, which accentuated his gauntness, was still running a temperature of 102°F, which contributed to the sweating, and was still on medication. He was asked whether he wanted to cancel the first debate, but he declined saying he did not want to be seen as a coward. He refused make-up. His choice of a light-grey suit also made him blend into the background and exaggerated his pale appearance.

Seventy million viewers watched the debate. The general reaction was that the younger Kennedy had matched his more experienced opponent impressively. He would be on a roll all the way to Election Day. And he would be the youngest to win a presidential election.

Kennedy is credited as winning his six victories in southern states by controversially selecting Texan Lyndon Johnson as his vice-presidential running mate. Kennedy won Texas, the most valuable in terms of Electoral College votes, by less than 50,000. He won the northern state of Illinois by an even closer margin – just 9,000 in nearly 5 million votes cast – where deliberate electoral fraud in a few Chicago precincts are now thought to have tipped the balance. Nixon would have triumphed overall had he won those two states.

Kennedy had not originally wanted Johnson as his running mate and only offered him the ticket assuming he would turn it down. He had been astonished when Johnson accepted.

Did the legacy of the 1960 election have a longer impact? Nixon accepted the outcome, although he was heard to moan to guests at his Christmas party that year that the election had been stolen by Kennedy. He nursed a grudge against the Democratic Party for years. When he finally became president and was criticised for his Watergate plot, he cited the Kennedy precedent as justification. If the 1960 election had not been so tainted, might Watergate not have happened?

Kennedy, whose presidency was cut down by assassination, nearly did not even make it to his inauguration in January 1961. A plot to assassinate him following his election was foiled by luck and Kennedy's own predilections for constant press coverage.

In December 1960, while waiting for Inauguration Day on 20 January, Kennedy and his young family were staying at one of the clan's houses in Palm Beach, Florida. Richard Pavlick, a 73-year-old retired postal worker from New Hampshire, concocted a plan to rig up a bomb in his car, wait for Kennedy to emerge from the house and crash into the president-to-be's limousine and detonate the device.

He arrived outside the house on 11 December, and waited. He

had not, however, reckoned on Kennedy's obsession with maintaining a good press. A throng of photographers always congregated outside. Every time he emerged, he would bring wife Jackie and their two-week old baby John Jnr.

Pavlick had nothing against Kennedy's wife or baby, and kept waiting for a solo opportunity. Remarkably, he sat outside the house in his car for five successive days. He was eventually arrested on 15 December by a local police officer, not for his suspicious behaviour, but for a minor traffic violation. The bomb in his car was then discovered.

No one knows how many times Kennedy came close to being blown up during that week. But the fortnight-old baby John appears certain to have saved his life.

The botched break-in at the headquarters of the Democratic Party that was eventually to lead to the downfall of Richard Nixon nearly went undiscovered. On the night of 17 June 1972 – in the middle of the presidential election campaign – security guard Frank Wills discovered masking tape stuck over a door latch leading into the Watergate complex in Washington which housed the offices of Nixon's rivals. He assumed it had been put there by a shift worker to make it easier to get in and out of the building, so he tore it off and simply put it in his pocket.

He came across a second taped door lock inside but assumed it was part of the previous scam. He removed that one too, and went off for a snack with a colleague.

It was only when he returned nearly two hours later and found one of the doors that he had earlier cleared, re-taped, that he called the police. They discovered five intruders, who turned out to be equipped with bugging devices. Their identities, and the money they carried, would lead back to maverick secret service and White House connections and eventually to evidence of Nixon's own attempts to cover up his involvement in the skullduggery.

…And it had so nearly passed Frank Wills by.

The revelation that would lead to President Richard Nixon's downfall in the Watergate scandal – that he taped all his White House meetings – only emerged when an aide disclosed the fact to investigators on the assumption that they already had the information from other more senior White House staff.

Over a year after the botched break-in, Alexander Butterfield, Nixon's overseer of administration, was interviewed by Senate staff investigating the alleged White House connection. He was shown what he recognised to be a transcript of a Nixon meeting. He thought he was simply corroborating someone else's testimony about the existence of the taping system. Unbeknown to him, it was the first evidence the investigators had. They had been working on a hunch.

Three days later, Butterfield was subpoenaed to testify to the Senate committee in public and a stunned world learned the strangest secret of the Nixon White House.

At a point in the investigations when the trail appeared to be going cold, and against Nixon's protestations of ignorance and innocence, the discovery would reveal damning evidence of the President's involvement in covering up the break-in at the election headquarters of his opponents during the 1972 presidential election. The White House would endure a further 13 months of legal battles to prevent the tapes being divulged to prosecutors, but the game was up. In August 1974, Nixon became the first and, to date, only president to resign from office.

If Ronald Reagan had had an off day on 2 March 1987, he would have become the second president to be removed from office prematurely while still alive.

Six years into his presidency with two more still to go, the oldest president ever to take office – he was 16 days short of his 70th birthday at his inauguration – was giving increasing concern to his staff regarding his apparent declining mental capacities. (Famous for his slow, confused and work-shy style, Reagan was formally diagnosed with Alzheimer's disease five years after leaving the White House.) It emerged in 1999 that his new Chief of Staff, Howard Baker, issued an instruction to senior staff members that they should all observe the President carefully on that March day. If they agreed with Baker that the President was 'disoriented', he would consult lawyers with a view to invoking the Constitutional provisions allowing a president to be removed from office on the grounds of incapacity.

In the event, Reagan reportedly bounced into the Oval Office full of energy and vigour that day and in full control of his faculties. The issue of his mental competence was never raised again while he was in office.

Over half a century before both Nixon and Reagan, Woodrow Wilson, leader during the First World War, would have been America's first president to resign from office if he had been defeated in the November 1916 election. At a time when the victorious president had to wait until March the following year before being formally inaugurated, Wilson concocted a plan to ensure that he would not have to serve as a 'lame duck' president for four months when overseeing the war effort required concerted political leadership.

If he had lost the voting on 7 November, he would have appointed his Republican rival Charles Evans Hughes as his Secretary of State. Wilson and his vice-president would then have immediately resigned, and under the succession provisions of the Constitution at the time, the presidency would have formally devolved to...the Secretary of State. Hughes would quite legally have become president four months before he should ordinarily have done.

In the event, Wilson narrowly won the election, by only 600,000 votes in nearly 18 million, and carried on for a second four-year term.

On the death of Israel's first president Chaim Weizmann in 1952, Israeli leaders approached Albert Einstein and asked him to be their second president. He declined, giving as the only reason that he had no head for human problems.

Cuban revolutionary Fidel Castro could have been a professional baseball player in the United States had his trial as a 21-year-old with the Washington Senators in 1947 turned out differently. And America might have been spared decades of headaches too.

After the failure of the direct assault on Castro's regime in the Bay of Pigs fiasco in the spring of 1961, the Pentagon and CIA adopted an altogether different approach to undermine him. Had astronaut John Glenn not returned safely from the first attempt to put an American into orbit in February 1962, the authorities would have laid the blame on Cuban radio interference for the disaster. A Pentagon plan, disclosed in 1997, detailed how 'various pieces of evidence could be manufactured which would prove electronic interference by the Cubans'.

It is tantalising to speculate what the impact on world opinion would have been of such a space disaster. Would the Russians, themselves charging ahead in the space race, have been suspicious of their protégé and perhaps of future blackmail? It is now known from Soviet archives published in 2005 that they harboured doubts at the beginning about Castro's Marxist commitment and Nikita Khrushchev had accused the Cuban leader of dangerous 'adventurism'.

In the event, Glenn successfully orbited three times and returned to Earth quite safely.

The iconic end of the Cold War, the fall of the Berlin Wall on 9 November 1989, was accidentally precipitated by an offhand remark by an obscure official at the end of a dull press conference being held that evening.

All day, in response to growing street demonstrations, the ruling East German Politburo had been working to agree a temporary arrangement to allow emigration from the country. Guenter Schabowski, the Politburo's media spokesman, who had not been at the meeting which approved the new regulations, was handed the dense document just before the government's regular six o'clock televised press conference. Within it was an announcement that further details would be issued the following day explaining the procedures for people to apply to leave the country.

At the end of a turgid hour of questions, the travel permit issue was reached. Exhausted and visibly sweating under hot TV lights, Schabowski read the stiltedly-worded regulations out in full. He leaned back in his chair, expecting no questions.

A journalist asked when the rules would come into force. Schabowski, unfamiliar with the intentions, and forgetting the part referring to plans for an explanatory statement the next day, had to shuffle through his papers to re-find the document, scanned it and replied in an uncertain tone that 'as far as I know…this is immediate, without delay.'

Within five minutes of the end of the conference, an Associated Press story was interpreting the announcement as East Germany 'opening its borders'. By ten o'clock over a thousand East Berliners had gathered at a crossing point at Bornholmerstrasse in central Berlin. A state television announcement at 10.30pm that those wanting to travel needed nevertheless to apply in advance and that this could be done as soon as passport offices opened at the normal time the following morning, failed to stem the growing public excitement.

Events spiralled out of control. By eleven o'clock all the border crossings in Berlin were besieged. At 11.30pm, Lt Col Harald Jager, commander of the checkpoint on Bornholmerstrasse, decided to order his men to stop checking passports and let the crowd do what it wanted. By midnight, all the border crossings had been forced to open. The Wall was no more. After 28 years, a botched announcement by a tired and partly informed official had let the genie out of the bottle. What had been hurriedly put up over-night in 1961 had come down in a similar one-night event a generation later.

On the 10th anniversary, Schabowski was reported as saying, 'It was one of many foul-ups in those days. I'm just happy that it went off without bloodshed.' Egon Krenz, the supreme leader then, maintained that the intention had been not the scrapping of the Wall but a calming of the emigration flood. Instead, the German Democratic Republic collapsed within 11 months. By October 1990, Germany was a reunited state.

If the Wall came down by accident, there is evidence to suggest that its creation was unwittingly prompted too, and not by the Communist regime but by the free West. The genesis of the Wall on 13 August 1961 was East Germany's chronic loss of people – mainly young professionals, the sort the young Communist republic could ill afford to lose – who were streaming across the open border in Berlin to freedom in the city's western zones still administered by the Allied occupying powers from the Second World War. On average, 2,000 every week were flooding through East Berlin. By mid August it had reached 1,500 a day.

As the exodus, and the sense of crisis, intensified the East got some odd signals from the West. President Kennedy had sympathised with Soviet leader Khrushchev in private about the problem, and three weeks before the Wall went up, on 25 July, gave a television address in which he emphasised that America would protect its position in Berlin but significantly said nothing about guaranteeing free access between the East and Western zones of the city.

Even more pointedly, five days later, the chair of the influential

Senate Foreign Relations Committee, William Fulbright, said publicly, 'I don't understand why the East Germans don't close the border because I think they have a right to close it.'

The Soviet and German authorities, struggling to contend with their crisis, could have been forgiven for reading into these statements hints that America would not forcefully resist the move they eventually made. And, when they did, their assumptions proved right.

3

History's Tricks – Accidents, Illnesses and Assassinations

Charles I, whose decisions polarised England between royalty and parliament and led to the Civil War, and whose disastrous reign ended in his beheading in 1649, should never have been king at all.

A weak, indecisive and stubborn character, he had been backward as a child (he did not talk until he was four or walk until seven). He had few attributes to mark him out as a good candidate for the throne. His personal weaknesses contributed heavily to the lack of political tact he showed in his rule and he created for himself many of the problems of his times.

He only became heir to the throne when his elder brother by six years, Henry, Prince of Wales, died from typhoid at the age of 18 in 1612. Henry, by contrast, was intelligent, learned and responsible – except, perhaps, for his choice of exercise: according to some accounts, he contracted the disease after going for a swim in the polluted Thames. That swim would have catastrophic consequences for Britain's history when Charles found himself elevated to the throne on the death of his father James I in 1625, still only 24.

Within two years he was at war with both Spain and France, which began the sorry tale of his prolonged fight with parliament over raising the taxes to pay for the conflicts, and which were to lead inexorably to civil war.

The madness of King George III (1760-1820) was

probably entirely avoidable, scientists in the United States concluded in 2005.

George was renowned for his abstemious approach to dining. He was always worried about getting fat, took a lot of exercise, often eating little more than boiled eggs or bread and butter with a cup of tea, which he would consume while pacing up and down. He rarely held state dinners or dined with his ministers. Court life has been described as 'intensely dull'.

According to a research team led by Dr Bruce Spiegelman from Harvard Medical School, the disease which afflicted him, porphyria, a hereditary complaint, has been found to be aggravated by low intake of carbohydrates and sugars which triggers a particular protein to become overactive and cause the mental instability. Said Dr Spiegelman, 'We have explained how porphyria symptoms can [be] triggered by fasting, and why they can be treated by feeding carbohydrates and glucose.'

Ironically, it would seem, George's frugal diet and concern for his health appears to have been precisely what ended up derailing him.

In contrast, historian nutritionists in 1989 concluded that Henry VIII's reign might have been a more stable affair had he eaten his vegetables. That might then have led to avoiding the break with Rome and Britain remaining a Catholic country.

The almost complete absence of vitamins in Henry's diet, which consisted pretty much entirely of meat and alcohol, fuelled his famously erratic mood swings. He is more likely to have died of scurvy brought on by malnutrition than the usually suspected causes, gout or syphilis. The puffy face of his later portraits, and descriptions of his foul breath and 'fungus legs' are classic symptoms of scurvy.

Had he eaten better, Britain's historic links with the pope may have turned out very differently indeed.

Had Franklin D. Roosevelt not been disastrously mistreated when he first developed polio, he might have been spared the lifelong crippling that the disease caused him. He could have lived a healthier, and longer, life and thus had a stronger impact on the peace settlement at the end of the Second World War.

The symptoms appeared when he was on a lakeside holiday with his family in 1921, when he was a 39-year-old ex-Senator and Assistant Secretary for the Navy. After a swim he developed severe leg pains. The family doctor recommended a celebrated surgeon, who coincidentally was vacationing nearby, to see him. Having never heard of polio being contracted in a person so old – it is almost always a disease of young children – the surgeon misdiagnosed the complaint as a lesion of the spine and recommended 'vigorous' massage of the limbs, just about the worst treatment possible for the early stages of polio. He underwent the treatment for two whole weeks before the Roosevelt family got a second opinion from an expert who immediately diagnosed polio.

The massaging was to cause permanent paralysis of Roosevelt's legs and although he learned to stand with metal callipers to hide his ailment in public – few outside the family and presidential circle ever knew of his disability – it effectively confined him to a wheelchair for the rest of his life.

The added irony of his plight is that in 80 per cent of cases, polio passes, causing no permanent damage. The treatment Roosevelt received from the unknowing doctor changed that for him.

The historic consequences may have been profound. As US President throughout the Second World War, his frailties increased as the conflict neared its end. For the last year, when crucial political confrontations with the Soviet Union set the course for the post-war territorial settlements, many historians see Roosevelt's failing health as a crucial factor in weakening

America's resilience against Stalin's demands as the victorious powers tussled over the fate of the Fascist empires. By the Yalta Conference of the 'Big Three' in February 1945 he was virtually a dead man standing, and historians universally judge Stalin to have come out on top in the negotiations. Two months later, Roosevelt was dead, aged just 63. Churchill, then already 70, in contrast would live another two decades.

The baby that would eventually rule as Queen Victoria, was nearly shot by a bird-hunting boy when just seven months old. On Christmas Day 1819 she was being cared for by a nurse at Woolbrook Cottage at Sidmouth where her parents, the Duke and Duchess of Kent, were holidaying. A shot broke the nursery window, and a bullet whistled close enough to the child's head to tear the sleeve of her shawl. The boy responsible had been taking pot shots at sparrows noisily chattering outside.

In later life, there would be as many as seven attempts to assassinate her as queen.

Had it not been for a small act of kindness, history would be recording Sir Robert Peel as the second British prime minister to have been assassinated. At the peak of his powers, he escaped being shot in January 1843 when the would-be assassin, Daniel MacNaghten, shot Peel's Private Secretary, Edward Drummond, as he walked near the Admiralty in Whitehall in the mistaken belief that he was shooting the Prime Minister. Drummond died of his injuries five days later.

The mistaken identity arose because when Peel had become prime minister two years earlier, he decided not to move into the prime minister's official residence at 10 Downing Street but remain in his own house which was conveniently located in nearby Whitehall Gardens. Peel had lent No. 10 to Drummond. MacNaghten had been staking out Downing Street for weeks and concluded that the man he saw regularly coming and going was Peel.

Lloyd George, prime minister during the First World War, escaped what is perhaps the most bizarre assassination plot against a British politician. Police arrested an odd group of radical extremists in Derby in January 1917, led by a 50-year-old second-hand clothes shop owner, Alice Wheeldon, her two daughters and her son-in-law, a chemist. Wheeldon was undoubtedly a fanatical suffragette, angry that the war had put an end to the campaign for women's votes.

The family devised a plan to kill Lloyd George while he was playing golf. They would shoot him with darts tipped with the deadly poison curare. The scheme unravelled when they chose the gunman who would actually do the shooting. He turned out to be an anti-subversion secret service agent, one of a pair who had infiltrated the group.

They were tried at the Old Bailey in March. After a five-day trial, the jury took just half an hour to convict. They were sentenced to varying terms of prison, Alice Wheeldon getting the highest penalty of 10 years.

Quite how the secret service had cottoned on to this nondescript group far away in the East Midlands has never been explained. An intriguing alternative theory is that the plot was an inside job sponsored by maverick elements within the establishment. The other agent who had befriended the group never appeared as a witness at the trial, and 10 years later was incarcerated in a mental asylum.

Lloyd George treated the whole affair casually. He ordered Wheeldon's release before the year ended. She died in February 1919 during the mass influenza epidemic which struck after the war.

A British doctor's misdiagnosis may have contributed to the sequence of events that would lead to the First World War. Sir Morell Mackenzie, an eminent throat expert, was asked in 1887 to examine the German Crown Prince Frederick, who had married the eldest daughter of Queen Victoria. The Prince was suspected of suffering from throat cancer, but Mackenzie, despite three examinations, was adamant that there was no malignancy. No action was therefore taken.

Months later, it became apparent that Frederick was indeed suffering from cancer, which by then had reached an inoperable stage. Two months afterwards, the reigning German Kaiser died and Fredrick succeeded to the throne – but ruled for only 99 days before dying in June 1888.

That left the way open for his son, Kaiser Wilhelm, whose erratic and bombastic reign destabilised European politics and did more than anything else to create the frictions that culminated in the outbreak of war in 1914.

Had his father's cancer been spotted earlier, who knows how long a reign Frederick might have had and what impact that might have had in producing an alternative set of events to those which unfolded?

The assassination that directly triggered the First World War, the killing of Austrian Archduke Franz Ferdinand while visiting Sarajevo on 28 June 1914, succeeded because of a driver's wrong turn and a scarcely credible coincidence.

The royal entourage from the city railway station to the town hall was the target of seven Serbian nationalist terrorists. Of the potential assassins lining the route, two found themselves in awkward positions in the crowd which prevented them from firing their weapons and two lost their nerve. The fifth managed to lob a bomb that bounced off the Archduke's car and exploded underneath the third vehicle in the convoy, injuring an officer. When the Archduke arrived at the town hall and learned of the outrage, he reacted with fury at this insult from the city, abandoned the reception formalities and asked to be driven to the hospital to see his wounded staff.

The eventual assassin, Gavrilo Princip, had heard the explosion, assumed the plot had worked and had taken himself off to a café on a street corner. The drivers of the royal cars had not been briefed of the change of destination. They drove the planned parade route along the riverside Appel-Quai back towards the station. The lead car took a tight turn off into a narrow street and the driver of the Archduke's car followed. When told this was not the way to the hospital, he stopped and began to reverse slowly out of the street. It happened to be the precise street corner on which Princip was sitting drinking his celebratory coffee.

Princip looked up, saw the Archduke barely yards away and walked over and fatally shot him. His aimed a second shot at the Army Chief of Staff, but a well-meaning rescuer tried to grab his arm and the bullet instead hit the Archduke's wife, Countess Sophie, who also died.

Within a month the Austrians, who blamed Russia for supporting the Serbs, had declared war on the Tsar. Their allies, Germany, also declared war on Russia, leading its ally, France, to declare war on Germany. Britain, as allies of France and Russia, followed suit. The 'Great War' would last for four years and lead to nine million deaths.

Emily Davison, the suffragette who died when she ran in front of the royal horse during the 1913 Epsom Derby may have achieved her lasting fame by sheer accident. An episode that has been portrayed as a deliberate suicide in the cause of women's votes may actually have been a ghastly error of judgement.

Intriguing evidence surfaced in 1986 in the form of personal possessions kept by the family's solicitor who represented them at the inquest. Amongst the papers was a telling item which casts doubt on the suicide theory: she was carrying a return rail ticket from Epsom back to Victoria, suggesting she had intended to go home that night.

The royal jockey, Herbert Jones, always doubted that Davison intended to bring his horse down. He is said to have been haunted by her look of surprise seconds before the collision. He was sure that she had misjudged the situation, and assumed that all the field had passed her at Tattenham Corner, but the deceptive rising ground obscured a bunch of stragglers, including his mount.

What may have been intended then simply as a public walk-on demonstration secured for Davison, perhaps more by luck than judgement, her immortal place in history.

At Abraham Lincoln's second inauguration in March 1865 a young man broke through the police ranks and almost reached the President. Police had been on the alert as a similar attempt had been made to disrupt Lincoln's first inaugural four years earlier. They apprehended the man and detained him for questioning. They let him go after deciding he was quite harmless. The man was John Wilkes Booth, who was to assassinate Lincoln six weeks later.

Lincoln almost decided not to go to the theatre in Washington the night he was assassinated in April 1865. Although it was Good Friday, he had worked a full day, starting at 8 o'clock, with a Cabinet meeting at 11 that lasted three hours, continual meetings in between (it was only five days after the Confederate surrender and the end of the Civil War) and he made a visit to the War Department in the afternoon.

Lincoln tried to get out of the evening engagement, to Ford's Theatre in the heart of town. He was tired and had seen the play before. One of the main reasons for him originally having to go – because Mrs Lincoln had invited Civil War hero General Grant and his wife to accompany them – was no longer an issue. Grant had sent his regrets during the day as he was going out of town on an afternoon train to visit his children in New Jersey.

But Mrs Lincoln had set her heart on the outing. He decided he could not pull out. 'It has been advertised that we will be there,' he told a bodyguard. 'I cannot disappoint the people'.

Grant's decision to cancel saved his own life. The plot against Lincoln was to have included him as a target. He later became president himself four years later. So America nearly lost two presidents that night at the theatre.

Lincoln would not have been the first American president to be assassinated had it not been for an incredible, and inexplicable, piece of fortune for Andrew Jackson 30 years before.

In the first ever attempt on a president's life, Jackson, who had been president for nearly six years, was shot at twice by a gunman as he left the Capitol building in January 1835. Richard Lawrence, a mentally unstable house painter, approached to within 13 feet of the President and fired. While the percussion cap exploded, it did not set off the gunpowder. As Jackson lunged forward to tackle the gunman, Lawrence fired a second gun at point blank range. This, too, failed to fire properly.

When his guns were later examined, firearms experts found both to be in perfect working order. They put the odds of both guns failing in succession at one in 125,000. Lawrence was later acquitted on the grounds of insanity and confined to an asylum until his death a quarter of a century later.

It was not the first remarkable escape for Jackson. He had carried a musket ball near his heart since a duel fought 23 years before he became president. It was so close that doctors refused to operate. His opponent in the duel, Charles Dickinson, reckoned to be one of America's foremost marksmen, had aimed directly for Jackson's heart but had been misled by Jackson's unusual skinniness and his wearing of an oversized coat. Dickinson had hit exactly where he had thought he wanted, but the coat concealed the true position of Jackson's frame. It missed by a fraction of an inch. Jackson's shot, incidentally, killed Dickinson.

Two small, but highly consequential decisions, put paid to William Henry Harrison, who has the distinction of being the shortest-serving president in US history – just 31 days.

A military hero of the Indian wars, born in a log cabin and elected in 1840 on a campaign ticket emphasising his personal strength of character, Harrison was the oldest person before Ronald Reagan to win the office, at 68. He delivered what still remains the longest inauguration speech ever, taking an hour and 40 minutes, did so on a freezing March day in 1841 and, to continue the theme of his stamina, decided against wearing a coat, hat or gloves.

He caught a cold that developed into pneumonia. Exactly a month after his inauguration, he was dead.

The second American president to be assassinated, James Garfield, died because an innovative metal detector invented by Alexander Graham Bell with which he tried to locate the bullet, failed to work – because no one knew that doctors had laid the President on a coiled spring mattress.

Garfield was shot on 2 July 1881, by a crazed gunman in Washington's main railway station, barely four months after becoming president. A bullet was lodged somewhere in his body but, despite numerous probes inside the wound, doctors were unable to find it. They feared to operate in case there had been damage to vital organs.

Although in great pain, after a few days Garfield was stable (he did not in fact die until 19 September, 11 weeks and several botched intrusive procedures later). Bell was intrigued by the case of the 'unlocatable' bullet. He brought to the White House a prototype device that he had been developing as an offshoot of his telephone and which he claimed was capable of detecting metal through electric currents.

Bell had already tested the machine with Civil War veterans who carried bullets in their bodies and it had successfully found the embedded metal. The President's doctors enthusiastically let Bell try it out on Garfield. It unexpectedly failed. Unknown to everyone, the President was lying on a newfangled coiled spring mattress, which disrupted the signal.

Franklin D. Roosevelt, who set a record for American presidents by winning four straight elections and serving more than 12 years in office, nearly did not serve a single day. Two weeks before his first inauguration in March 1933, while on holiday in Miami, he narrowly avoided assassination in a gun attack that saw the would-be assassin fire off five shots, all of which hit someone near the President, with one killing the Mayor of Chicago who was standing right beside him.

Guiseppe Zangara, an Italian bricklayer, somehow missed the President completely.

The assassination of John F. Kennedy in Dallas in November 1963 is replete with conspiracy theories over who might have been responsible. One of the biggest obstacles to probing deeper into the incident is the paucity of photographic evidence. Apart from one moving-film sequence of the killing taken by a bystander, there is hardly any other visual material.

One of the curious, and still unexplained, reasons for this is that the press corps vehicle, which had always been positioned directly in front of the President's car to help photographers get the best angles, was on this occasion consigned right to the back of the 14-car cavalcade (even though officially it was designated to be in sixth place).

From their position, none of the pressmen covering the trip were able to provide any visual evidence which might have been crucial in the investigation. Bad luck, or bad intent?

Kennedy's prodigious womanising only emerged publicly in the years after his assassination. His philandering, however, seems very likely to have contributed directly to his death in Dallas.

According to Washington investigative reporter Seymour Hersh's 1997 exposé, *The Dark Side of Camelot*, Kennedy severely tore a groin muscle while frolicking with one of his illicit partners during a vacation in late September 1963. Doctors ordered him to wear a stiff canvas shoulder-to-groin body brace that locked him rigidly upright. This, and the back brace he already regularly wore because of an old football injury which had been exacerbated during war service, made it impossible for him to bend in reaction to the assassin's first bullet. This hit him in the throat but was not a fatal shot. His head remained upright and did not move. The second, deadly strike, blew his brains out.

The very first assassination of an American president that might have been caught on film, of William McKinley at the Pan-American Exposition in Buffalo, New York, in September 1901, was missed through unlucky timing. The Edison Company had been filming the President on the day of his visit and was changing reels when word spread that McKinley had been shot. They had missed the actual shooting. All they could do was to film scenes showing the crowd's reaction to the outrage.

Charles de Gaulle was a frequent target for assassination

throughout his presidency of France because of his policy on Algeria, first resisting the independence movement and fighting a civil war there between 1954 and 1962, and then being regarded as a traitor by French Algerians after he agreed to independence. A shadowy organisation of former settlers, the OAS, plotted dozens of attempts to kill him in revenge.

One source suggests there were no fewer than 31 documented attempts on his life. Most were gun attacks and, as de Gaulle always travelled in a bulletproof car, were less dangerous than they looked. One famous attack in August 1962 in a Paris suburb deposited 14 bullets holes in the presidential limousine and shot out two of the four tyres.

He came closer to death when the plotters used explosives. The narrowest escape came by sheer luck. In July 1966, de Gaulle was being driven to Orly Airport. His car passed a parked vehicle on the Boulevard Montparnasse which was packed with a ton of explosives. It did not go off because there was no one to prime the bomb. Those behind the attack, students from an extreme right-wing group pressing for the preservation of French Algeria, had gone off to commit a robbery to get funds to escape abroad, and had been arrested during that crime.

It was the last known attempt to kill de Gaulle.

Leon Trotsky, organiser of the Red Army that helped Lenin to success in the Communist revolution in Russia, was assassinated in Mexico in August 1940, 13 years after being forced into exile after he fell out with Stalin. It was the second attempt on his life that year. The previous May, he had survived an attack by Stalin's henchmen when his bedroom was sprayed with 73 bullets – he escaped without a scratch.

He was eventually done for by a lone assassin who had befriended him over recent months. He buried an ice pick in Trotsky's skull. He had been let through the usual security checks because Trotsky's bodyguards had been busy belatedly bolting the stable door after the earlier attack: they had been installing an up-to-date security system.

A momentary lapse of concentration by Winston Churchill a decade before he was called upon to be prime minister, almost robbed Britain of its wartime leader.

In December 1931, during a lecture tour in New York, Churchill was nearly killed when knocked down by a car as he absent-mindedly stepped off a curb to cross Fifth Avenue, having looked the wrong way to check for traffic.

He had forgotten that Americans drove on the opposite side of the road and was hit by the vehicle, which was travelling at nearly 35mph from the other direction. He suffered serious head and thigh injuries and spent nearly three weeks in bed recuperating. But he fully recovered, to history's good fortune.

The incident did have its silver lining. He made £600 (about £30,000 in modern values) from an article he wrote about it for the *Daily Mail* the following January.

While serving as a First World War major on the Western Front in 1915, Churchill miraculously escaped death by just 15 minutes. He was ordered to meet a car sent by his Corps Commander, General Haking, on 26 November, which meant a three-mile walk across muddy countryside to make the rendezvous. He left in good time, and shortly before an artillery barrage opened up targeting his sector. When he reached the appointed spot, he learned that the firing had driven off his pick-up. A staff officer told him that the meeting could take place later as it 'was only about things in general and that another day would do equally well.'

A grumpy Churchill tramped the three miles back to his company headquarters to discover that a quarter of an hour after he had left his dugout, a shell had landed a few feet from where he had been sitting, destroying the shelter and killing the orderly who was inside. He later wrote, 'When I saw the ruin I was not so angry with the General after all.'

Churchill's own military valet also had reason to be thankful. Churchill had taken him with him for the meeting 'to carry my coat.'

Churchill often reflected on this near-death episode and the effect of chance. 'You may walk to the right or to the left of a particular tree, and it makes the difference whether you rise to command an Army Corps or are sent home crippled or paralysed for life.'

A Battle of Britain veteran revealed in 2000 how he saved Churchill from being shot by his own wife during a pre-war visit to an RAF station at Croydon in 1939. Clementine Churchill was being shown around the cockpit of a fully-armed Gloster Gladiator fighter plane. Winston was bending down in front of one of the guns when, according to James Sanders, Clementine's host, her finger went unwittingly to press the firing button.

'I knocked her hand away to stop her,' he recalled. A year later, Churchill was prime minister.

Had anything happened to Churchill in the early years of the war, it is conceivable that Britain would have been run by a South African. The diaries of one of Churchill's Private Secretaries, Sir John Colville, regarded as the most intimate inside account of the war premiership, relate how in October 1940, after the invasion scare appeared to be over but before the winter Blitz descended, insiders in Downing Street seriously contemplated the chances of General Jan Christiaan Smuts, the Prime Minister of South Africa, who Churchill trusted for military advice and had invited into the Imperial War Cabinet (just as Lloyd George had done in the First World War).

Smuts' reputation, with his unparalleled experience of the workings of the war cabinet, stood high in London, and the idea of a Dominion head leading Britain was seen as the much-needed proof of the unity of the worldwide British Commonwealth at a time when Britain stood alone.

The seed of the idea, Colville suggests, was quietly fed into the King's circle through the Queen, whom Colville's mother knew, and other royal intimates. Two weeks later, Colville recorded in his diary that Queen Mary had been very taken by the idea and passed it on to George V, who also reacted favourably. As history turned out, the plan was never needed.

Although such an idea may sound far-fetched at this distance in time, the period was one of gigantic and unprecedented change. Barely four months earlier, as France tottered towards an armistice with Germany, the British Cabinet offered France a formal legal and political merger with the United Kingdom to try to stem defeat across the Channel. The French, in disarray, could not organise themselves in time to accept it. In such times, anything could seem a possibility.

Communism may have had its origins in an irritable skin disease. Writing in the *British Journal of Dermatology* in 2007, medical historian Professor Sam Shuster reported that there was credible evidence that Karl Marx suffered from a skin disease which can create a severe psychological disorder, fostering feelings of exploitation and alienation. He theorised that the affliction could very likely have given a significant push to the direction of thought Marx took which ended up with him inventing the theory that underpinned communism.

The researcher believed him to have been suffering from hidradenitis suppurativa, a repulsively messy disorder of the sweat glands that produces boils and pus-oozing spots. Although it was unclear when he first began to be affected by the disease, the symptoms were in evidence by 1864, when Marx was 46 years old and researching in the British Museum in London for his major work, *Das Kapital*, that lays out the conceptual theory of communism and which was published in 1867.

So it may have been all the misery, exasperation and feeling of oppression from these bodily ills that could, the medic suggests, have been the main driving force which created the state of mind that dreamt up a system of politics which was to plague hundreds of millions of people's lives in the century to come.

British novelist Arnold Bennett died of typhoid in 1931 after a trip to Paris. He contracted the disease there from drinking a glass of local tap water. According to the most popular account, he had done so in order to demonstrate that the water in France was perfectly safe.

The last words of Albert Einstein, perhaps the greatest scientific mind of all time, are unknown as he uttered them in German as he passed away in 1955 and the nurse who was with him when he died did not speak the language.

The *Titanic* disaster might have been prevented had a member of the crew not forgotten to hand over the key to his locker.

Second Officer David Blair was removed from the ship's roster at the last minute before the *Titanic*'s departure from Southampton in April 1912. In the haste of being replaced, Blair failed to pass to his replacement the key to the crow's nest locker which held the binoculars vital for the lookouts.

After the disaster, which cost 1,522 lives, one of the surviving lookouts, Fred Fleet, giving evidence to the US inquiry, confirmed that they did not have any binoculars on the voyage. Had they done so, he testified, they could have seen the iceberg earlier. When the chairman of the inquiry asked, 'How much earlier?' the lookout replied, 'Well, enough to get out of the way.'

The key, which saved the life of Blair, was kept as a memento. His descendants put it up for auction in 2007. It fetched £90,000.

The world's worst air disaster, the collision of two Boeing 747 jumbo jets at Tenerife's Los Rodeos airport in the Canary Islands on a Sunday evening in March 1977, was indirectly the result of a minor terrorist act. A small bomb planted by a group campaigning for independence for the Canaries had exploded at midday at the airport on neighbouring Las Palmas causing the airport to be closed. All flights were diverted to the Tenerife.

This resulted in the airport becoming hopelessly overcrowded. Fog descended during the afternoon which hampered operations further. The collision, between an American Pan Am 747 and a Dutch KLM jumbo, happened because of confusion about the aircrafts' whereabouts in the fog. The Dutch plane, trying to take off, careered into the American 747 that was taxiing and had unknowingly strayed on to the main runway. Five hundred and eighty-three passengers died. There were just 70 survivors – all from the American craft.

Accident investigators of the 1998 crash of a Swissair flight from New York off Canada's Nova Scotia coast recommended one crucial change to in-flight procedures. They urged that airlines should drastically shorten the checklist that pilots are required to follow to detect the source of cabin fires. They discovered that at the time of the crash, Swissair's checklist took 30 minutes to go through. The flight had crashed only 20 minutes from the first signs of smoke on board.

Air Canada's flight 143 from Montreal to Edmonton in

July 1983 nearly ended in catastrophe when it ran out of fuel midway through its journey. Pilots glided the Boeing 767 for more than 100 miles before making a successful emergency landing on a disused airstrip near Winnipeg, narrowly missing a motor racing event that was being held there.

Investigators discovered that the ground crew had got their metric and imperial measurements mixed up. Instead of loading the plane with 22,300kg of fuel (or 49,060 imperial pounds), they had only loaded 22,300 pounds.

Air Canada had just taken delivery of its first four 767s. The craft was the first of the fleet to be calibrated in metric units. Up until then, all the airline's planes were measured in imperial – and the crew carelessly forgot.

The beaching on to rocks on the Cornish coast of the 1,840 ton cargo ship *RMS Mülheim* in March 2003 was caused, the accident investigators found, by the captain catching his trousers on a control lever, falling over and knocking himself unconscious. He was the only person on the helm at the time. By the time he had recovered consciousness, the vessel was aground on the rocky coastline near Sennen. She lost up to half her cargo, which washed out to sea. The ship was a total wreck, and eventually broke up seven months later.

In the most serious of more than 20 incidents since the Second World War in which American nuclear weapons have either been involved in major accidents or fires which released radioactive material or where missiles have actually been lost, a B-52 bomber carrying two 24-megaton nuclear weapons broke up in mid-air over Goldsboro, North Carolina, in January 1961, four days after the inauguration of President Kennedy. One of the bombs fell into a marshy area and has never been recovered. The other crash-landed and scattered across a wide area. When it was recovered and analysed, scientists found that five out of the six safety devices had failed. Only a single switch had prevented the bomb from detonating. The weapon was 2,000 times more powerful than that dropped on Hiroshima.

The US air force lost two F-16 fighter planes to crashes in the space of 30 months in 1991–93 because the pilot had encountered difficulties in controlling the craft while using his 'piddle-pack' to urinate during the flight. Each craft cost $18 million.

San Francisco's Golden Gate bridge was on the point of collapse during its first severe weather test during a storm in December 1951. In the early evening 70mph winds caused the deck of the bridge to sway 24ft from side to side and 5ft up and down. The main cables, which in normal conditions are 32 inches apart, were rubbing together.

Calculations done at the time indicated that had the wind lasted for just another 25 minutes, the structure would probably have given way. The bridge was later strengthened with 250 seven-ton steel braces under the roadway.

It was the first time the bridge had had to close due to weather since its opening in 1937. It has done so only twice since.

Another curious possibility surrounds the bridge's famous rust red colour. It was chosen because it blended best with the surrounding scenery. If the US Navy had had its way, the bridge would have been painted in bright yellow and black stripes to improve visibility for shipping.

As many as 6,000 people died in a mass poisoning in Iraq in 1971 because vital labels on imported contaminated grain seed warning against human consumption were printed only in English and Spanish.

The cargo of American barley and Mexican wheat had been exported to Iraq for use as seed only. To ensure it was not eaten, it had been sprayed with mercury, and dyed bright pink as a warning. The sacks were labelled in the languages of the exporting countries but not in Arabic. The consignment was quickly stolen after it had been offloaded in Basra, and sold to the poor.

The full scale of the tragedy only emerged two years later after an American investigative journalist pieced together the epidemic of mercury poisoning which had followed. The final death toll, from hospital reports, appeared to be at least 6,000, with more than 100,000 more suffering disabilities ranging from blindness, deafness, brain damage and paralysis. No one was ever prosecuted.

The West African state of Benin had its entire air force destroyed in 1988 by a single errant golf shot.

Metthieu Boya, a ground technician and keen golfer, was practising on the airfield during a lunchtime break when he sliced a drive. The ball struck the windscreen of a jet fighter that was preparing to take off, causing it to career into the country's other four jets neatly lined up by the runway. All five aircraft were write-offs.

Winchester cathedral had to be saved from destruction in the early 20th century by a deep-sea diver. In 1905, the authorities discovered that the foundations of the medieval cathedral, which was begun in the 11th century, were resting on tree trunks that, in turn, were lying on a waterlogged peat bed.

The operation to strengthen the base before the structure collapsed centred on a solitary diver – William Walker – who was hired to descend into the watery bowels every day for nearly six years to dig out the peat. With 250 helpers above ground, it was replaced with brickwork, 115,000 concrete blocks and 25,000 bags of cement. A statue to the 'Winchester Diver' stands in the cathedral commemorating the bizarre feat.

4

The Fog of War

The divorce in 1152 of Eleanor of Aquitaine, Queen of France and one of history's most powerful women leaders, and King Louis VII led to an Anglo-French war that lasted 301 years. She had immediately married the English King, Henry II, a bare six weeks later, gifting into our hands her ancestral lands across a swathe of central France. This infuriated Louis as it required him to acknowledge Henry as Duke of Aquitaine which occupied nearly a quarter of all France.

The reason for the divorce? When Louis had returned from the Crusades, Eleanor objected to him having shaved off his beard, which she thought made him look ugly. When he refused to grow it back, she split. It would lead to three centuries of running conflict between the two countries, including the Hundred Years' War. Peace and stability were not restored until 1453 after the Battle of Rouen, when the English had eventually been driven out of all of France except Calais.

A 12-year war, the War of the Oaken Bucket, was sparked between two of northern Italy's states in 1325 when a regiment of soldiers from Modena crossed the border into Bologna – to steal a bucket. Thousands died before peace was restored. Today, the stolen bucket can still be seen in the bell tower of Modena cathedral.

At a perilous moment in its history, the fate of England was decided by the fortunes of the weather. The 130-strong fleet of the Spanish Armada which attempted to invade the southern English coast in 1588 was defeated not by any force of arms but by the vagaries of the British climate. The English fleet in fact sank only one enemy ship, and then ran out of ammunition.

After an unscathed drive up the Channel, winds blew the Armada out into the North Sea and prevented a landing – precisely at the moment when the defending fleet had exhausted its ammunition supply. As the Armada made its way home around Scotland and Ireland, a hurricane-force storm then wrecked it. Only 65 ships – half the original fleet – straggled back to Spain. For good reason, the celebratory medal struck by the English authorities was emblazoned with the motto, 'God blew, and they were scattered'.

A smallpox epidemic curiously ravaged the eastern seaboard of America throughout the War of Independence, from 1775 when it began until 1782, the year after the British were defeated and had left for home. Historians still dispute today whether Britain had deliberately spread the disease as an early form of biological warfare. The colonists were convinced of it.

The actual evidence is unclear, although the British army was known to be inoculating its troops. It could be just as likely that the disease was transported naturally through the large numbers of troops brought across from Europe. Whatever the cause, the disease played havoc with military operations. It frequently reduced available troop numbers to a third of the notional complement. In June 1776, one of the Continental Army leaders, John Adams, wrote to a friend that smallpox was 'ten times more terrible than Britons, Canadians and Indian together.' Thousands

71

of soldiers succumbed, and it may have contributed to the war lasting much longer than it needed to.

If it had been a deliberate ploy to wipe out the leadership of the American rebellion, the plan suffered from one unknown flaw. George Washington, commander-in-chief of the Continental Army, was immune to smallpox, having contracted it in his youth. He was able to lead from the front without any fears whatsoever.

Washington narrowly escaped injury many times during the War of Independence. He is reported to have had at least three horses shot from under him and his hat shot from his head. But one event, in the early stages of the war, on 7 September 1777, came remarkably close to snuffing out the future leader before any of his great military or political triumphs.

The episode only came to light in the 1940s when a document was unearthed in the Public Record Office in London. It was a description by Major Patrick Ferguson, a renowned sharpshooter and inventor of the light breech-loading rifle, who was in service during the war near Brandywine Creek where the opposing forces were at one of their closest points. He gave an account of an encounter with a rebel patrol, led by one officer wearing 'a remarkably large cocked hat' denoting a rank of high importance.

Ferguson, who had once scored a bull's eye at 100 yards demonstrating his rifle to King George III, recounted that 'I could have lodged half a dozen bullets in him,' but after initially intending to shoot when he was in range decided not to when they changed direction. 'It was not pleasant to fire at a man's back, so I let him alone.' Instead he shouted for their surrender, and they raced off to safety.

At the Battle of Brandywine Creek in the days that followed, Ferguson was wounded, taken to hospital and overheard a surgeon recounting his recent work dressing the wounds of captured rebel soldiers. The prisoners had told of Washington's pre-battle

THE FOG OF WAR

manoeuvres, and Ferguson realised that it had been Washington who had come within his sights.

Washington never knew how close he had come to being the victim of the British army's best marksman.

The Battle of New Orleans in early January 1815, the last engagement between British and American forces in the so-called War of 1812, was a victory for the defending Americans and made future President Andrew Jackson a national hero for leading the defence of the country's major southern port. The whole battle, however, ought never to have been fought.

It took place two weeks *after* the official peace treaty ending the war had been signed, on Christmas Eve 1814, in Ghent in modern Belgium. News was still on its way from Europe and too late to prevent the final encounter. Nearly a thousand men lost their lives in one of the most pointless battles in history.

The War of 1812 ended in farce. It had started in the same vein too. The main cause of friction lay in America's belief that Britain was trying, through naval blockades and restricting trade, to squeeze the life out of the new republic. America eventually declared war on 18 June 1812. It would not have degenerated into conflict had they given themselves a few more weeks.

Back in England, a new government under Lord Liverpool had taken office 10 days earlier after the assassination of Spencer Perceval. Liverpool was in favour of a more conciliatory approach to America. He had had one of the key reasons for the war removed by withdrawing controversial orders allowing the conscription of American nationals into the British navy.

The orders had been rescinded just the day before the American declaration of war. The Americans could not be aware of this as there was no way for the news to reach Congress before it voted for war. Three more weeks, and news of the British climb-down would have been known. The war would last two and a half years and cost nearly 4,000 lives.

Only the weather saved what is now the White House in Washington from deliberate destruction at the hands of British forces during the War of 1812 (which despite its name, lasted until January 1815). One of the most disreputable episodes of the conflict was the wholesale sacking of the American capital in August 1814. All the main public buildings were torched, including the Capitol, the seat of Congress, along with the Treasury, State Department, War Office and every book in the National Library.

The president's official home was also set on fire. It was saved by the fortuitous onset of a thunderstorm that put out the flames before the whole building could be destroyed. The modern White House building is still essentially the same structure. Until 1814 it was not actually white, but grey, the colour of the Virginian sandstone from which it was built. After the fire, it was painted white to cover up the smoke stains, and became familiarly known as the White House.

Had the president at the time been Thomas Jefferson and not the milder James Madison, St Paul's Cathedral in London might be a different building today.

Jefferson had left the presidency in 1809. After the Washington events, he wrote to his successor with a reprisal plan for the destruction wreaked on the national capital. He offered to organise to burn down St Paul's Cathedral and St James's Palace and presented a plan for doing so. The Madison administration, however, declined to antagonise the British any further.

Napoleon possibly lost the Battle of Waterloo because on the day of the final denouement he suffered an acute attack of hemorrhoids that stopped him from riding his horse and keeping up his usual mobile supervision of troop movements. It was the

THE FOG OF WAR

only time he had been prevented from directing his armies in the way he preferred.

He had suffered earlier during the campaign. Two days before, his doctors had lost the leeches used to relieve the pain and accidentally overdosed him with laudanum, from whose ill-effects he was still suffering on the morning of the battle.

According to some analyses of his decisions that day, Napoleon's delays in launching his opening assault had much to do with his indispositions: originally planned for 6am, then 9am, it did not actually start until nearly midday.

There might actually never have been the need for the Battle of Waterloo at all. Napoleon had tried to commit suicide over a year before, in April 1814, after surrendering to the Allies following the collapse of French forces and the occupation of Paris by the troops of Britain, Russia, Prussia and Austria.

Before the plans for exiling him to Elba had been settled, on 12 April he swallowed a vial of poison that he had carried with him since his retreat from Moscow. All it did was to give him a violent bout of hiccups, which caused him to vomit before the poison could do any harm.

The most infamous military debacle in the history of the British army – the Charge of the Light Brigade in October 1854 at the Battle of Balaclava during the Crimean War – hinged on a simple misunderstanding in orders which could have been cleared up easily had the two soldiers involved not been sworn enemies.

The charge against a Russian battery, down a narrow ravine flanked on both sides by heavy Russian forces, was suicidal. The order had not been to do that, but to head off some escaping Russian guns which the commander of the British forces, Lord Raglan, could see from his high position overlooking the field of battle, but which General Lucan, lower down, could not. They were in an entirely different direction to the ravine.

Raglan sent a messenger across to Lucan with the ambiguous order to 'prevent the enemy carrying off their guns'. The messenger happened to be his aide-de-camp, Captain Nolan, whom Lucan detested. The feelings were reciprocal. When Lucan, who could only see the valley ahead of him, and assuming the guns being referred to were those at the far end, queried the order, Nolan, who failed to see that he had misunderstood, thought he was simply being troublesome. He failed to clarify, repeated the order and departed.

Lucan passed the order on to his second in command, Lord Cardigan, who also queried it but Lucan could only reply that it was the commander-in-chief's order.

The brigade proceeded – they never actually charged – at a steady pace down the valley to oblivion towards guns that were never meant to be attacked. Nearly half the 675 men were killed or wounded and nearly all the horses.

But it did give rise to a good poem.

The leaders of the two rival Republics in the American Civil War, the President of the Northern Union, Abraham Lincoln, and Jefferson Davis, President of the secessionist Confederacy, were both born in Kentucky less than a hundred miles (and just eight months) apart.

Both their families migrated out of the state when the boys were young, Lincoln's family northward, to Indiana, Davis's southward, to Mississippi. Historians have often speculated that had the choices of their parents been reversed, the competing forces in the Civil War may well have had reversed leaders, with who knows what historical consequences. Might the Confederacy have just managed to win under the sharper political talents of Lincoln? Would Davis's authoritarian style have survived in the more challenging and competitive North? What momentous difference did the parochial choices of two families 50 years before have on American destiny?

The battle that turned out to be the most decisive engagement of the Civil War, the Battle of Gettysburg in 1863, began entirely by accident, and may have happened because of a newspaper advert. It was not a fight either side had planned.

Both forces, Union and Confederate, were widely scattered around the area in Pennsylvania. A rebel brigade commanded by Henry Heth had picked up a rumour that a supply of new boots lay in the town. One account has it that he got the information from picking up a stray copy of the local newspaper, the *Gettysburg Compiler,* where he saw an advert from a shoe store announcing the arrival of new stock. His troops were sorely in need of new footwear, having been marching for months.

Heth sought permission to go and get them. His commander, conscious of an order from General Lee not to engage the enemy in battle until the Confederate forces could be concentrated, had been cautious to avoid contact with the enemy. He refused Heth's request.

Had Heth not wanted those shoes so much, there would have been no battle at Gettysburg. But he did. Heth took his request up to the next level, to Major General Ambrose Hill, and convinced him that there were no enemy forces in the town. Asked if he had any objection, Hill said, 'None in the world.'

On 1 July, around 8 o'clock in the morning, Heth blundered into a Union cavalry unit and as hostilities broke out both sides rushed reinforcements to converge on the town. In three days, the fate of the whole war was decided. It was the greatest and bloodiest battle fought on the North American continent – 90,000 Union troops pitched against 75,000 Confederates. A third of all those engaged were lost. The South suffered 28,000 casualties against the North's 23,000.

By late on 3 July, Lee was in retreat and although the war would go on for nearly two more years, he was never to regain the strategic initiative. He had been unable to pick his own moment for a decisive battle. A junior's hunt for some shoes had catapulted him into an engagement against his expressed instructions and it ended up losing the South the war.

The South, however, did come within 24 hours of entering the American capital a year later in July 1864 in the last major Confederate assault in their campaign to take the war into the north. The only reason why Washington escaped destruction was the mercenary greed of the officer in command of the invading forces.

Major General Jubal Early had dallied for a day at Frederick, Maryland, just 40 miles from Washington. It had become a successful practice of enemy troops to demand ransoms from communities they passed through to save their towns from being burned down. Early had made $20,000 (perhaps the equivalent of around $1 million in modern value) from the residents of nearby Hagerstown three days before. At Frederick he demanded $200,000. He had to wait an extra day as the townsfolk collected the cash together. That lost day allowed 8,000 northern troops to pour into the defences three miles outside the town at Monocacy Junction to block the road to Washington.

The Battle of Monocacy proved sufficient to drain the strength from Early's attack and, although victorious, and now within 12 miles of the capital, he had had enough, turned south and headed back home.

Had he not waited at Frederick, the path to the nation's capital would have been undefended, the northern government could well have been forced to flee and…who knows how that might have affected the tide of the war.

As a footnote, the residents of Frederick, who had had to borrow much of the ransom, diligently paid back their debt, eventually clearing it – in 1951, 87 years later.

The young Winston Churchill's exploits in the Boer War in South Africa made his reputation as a gung-ho celebrity, and helped him win his election to parliament within three months of his return to England at the age of just 25. He might never have made it, however, had it not been for an astonishing stroke of luck after his escape at the end of 1899 from a Boer prisoner-of-war camp in Pretoria.

He was 300 miles from the safety of the border with Portuguese East Africa – all hostile Boer territory. He had no map or compass, and could not speak Afrikaans or any other local language. After an all-night journey hitched on a goods train, he jumped from it as it neared its destination and headed towards some lights that turned out to be a coal mining settlement.

He knocked at the door of the house at the mine head, and having established the resident was English confessed who he was and that he was on the run. The man he had stumbled upon, John Howard, was the mine's manager. His had been the only British-occupied house for 20 miles around. He hid Churchill down the mine for two days before arranging another train trip across the border.

With a £25 bounty on his head – 'Dead or Alive' – any other house that Churchill had approached would more than likely have led to him being turned in by a patriotic Boer and being shot for treason.

The first major action of the First World War in Africa, a British amphibious invasion of German East Africa at Tanga in November 1914, ended in a humiliating defeat for the invaders, largely through the intervention of a swarm of bees.

The 8,000 troops under General Arthur Aitken faced a mere 1,000 Germans. But the defenders were vastly better prepared. And the invaders, all untrained Indian reservists, poorly coordinated – they spoke 12 languages amongst themselves – encountered a more threatening adversary. The gunfire had agitated large numbers of bee colonies containing thousands of aggressive African bees, which attacked the British force in large numbers.

Despite the numerical disadvantage, the German force easily repelled the British who suffered nearly 1,000 casualties, of whom 360 were killed. (Those not killed or wounded were severely stung by bees.) The Germans benefited too from thousands of rifles and machine guns left behind by the fleeing British, along with over half a million rounds of ammunition.

The German commander, Colonel Paul von Lettow-Vorbeck, established himself that day as a national hero. He would lead the German effort in Africa during the war, and never lost a battle throughout. Yet his first contact with a massively larger force could have been his last had it not been for the bees.

The winner of the Spanish Civil War in the late 1930s, Francisco Franco, who would rule Spain until his death in 1975, might not have made it as the nation's strongman if his chief rival had not been so obsessed with dressing up.

General Jose Sanjurjo died in an air crash in Portugal as he was returning to Spain to combine with Franco's forces at the start of the civil war in July 1936. The reason for the crash was his extraordinary amount of luggage. Against the advice of his pilot, Sanjurjo had crammed the small plane full of his ceremonial military uniforms. The pilot warned him the plane was too heavily loaded, but Sanjurjo, anticipating the role he would play, replied, 'I need to wear proper clothes as the new Caudillio of Spain.'

Franco was left with a clear run as leader when his other main rival also died in an air crash less than a year later.

Adolf Hitler was about to commit suicide after the first major setback in his political career, but was prevented from doing so by a well-meaning associate.

As a young rabble-rousing agitator in the chaotic post-First World War years in Munich, Hitler led the Nazi coup attempt against the Bavarian government in the so-called Beer Hall Putsch in November 1923. It failed amidst a shootout with the police which left 16 leading Nazis dead and Hitler injured with a dislocated shoulder from diving to the ground for safety. He was ushered away to a safe house owned by his close friend, Ernst Hanfstaengl.

When the police tracked him down two days later, Hitler became hysterical, pulled out his revolver and tried to shoot himself. Frau Hanfstaengl prised the gun from his hand and stopped him. The next time he would attempt it, in 1945, he would succeed – a world war and 55 million deaths later.

One authority estimates that Hitler survived at least 15 assassination attempts between 1938 and 1944, most with uncanny luck.

The first documented attempt, before Hitler became Chancellor, was by a disgruntled SS guard who in 1929 planted a remote-controlled bomb under the podium in the Berlin Sportsplast where Hitler was speaking. The plot failed when the guard felt the urge to go to the toilet during the speech and accidentally got locked in. He was unable to detonate his device.

Hitler was on the point of being overthrown by his army leaders twice during the Czech crisis of September 1938, once when the plotters planned to move when Hitler issued the definitive order for the invasion of Czechoslovakia – only to be thwarted by British Prime Minister Chamberlain's surprise announcement of his willingness to hold direct talks with Hitler; and second during the Chamberlain missions when Hitler rejected British offers for conciliation – only to be thwarted this time by the pressure put on Hitler from Mussolini, who persuaded Hitler to agree to the four-nation Munich conference which eventually settled the crisis. The army commander-in-chief, General Brauchitsch, was about to issue the order to depose Hitler on 28 September, but refused to do so before he had spoken with him. News of the Munich conference reached him as he was on his way to the Chancellery for the showdown.

The declaration of war in September 1939 alarmed sections of the German army. As plans developed during the autumn for the military attack on the West, so did renewed plotting to overthrow the Führer.

The first attempt was instigated after Hitler had decreed that the invasion of the West would start on 12 November. Four days before that was the annual marking of the 1923 Munich putsch. Hitler would deliver a major speech on the evening of 8 November in the city's Burgerbraukeller, the beer hall where the coup attempt had started.

A bomb was placed in a pillar at the back of the speakers' platform, timed to explode around 9.20 in the evening. Hitler was due to start his speech at 8pm, and usually spoke for two hours. The assassination would come at the peak of the address.

The hall was packed (it could hold 3,000) and Hitler did not start speaking until 8.10 because of the rapturous greetings. For no obvious reason, Hitler suddenly brought his speech to a hasty conclusion at 9.07, and, again against normal practice, rushed out of the building instead of conducting his usual prolonged departure shaking hands.

Eight minutes later, the bomb exploded. Seven of the audience near the stage were killed and 63 injured. Had Hitler been on the podium, he too would certainly have been amongst the dead.

(*There is controversy over this episode. Some evidence exists – from the carpenter who planted the bomb – that tends to another possible explanation: that the explosion was actually a Hitler-inspired attempt to kill off some of his unreliable army chiefs who were in the audience.*

Hitler had been angry at their resistance to his war plans against the West. The bomber was caught but never tried. This version would explain Hitler's uncharacteristic behaviour that night, but he seemed genuinely surprised and shocked when news of the attack was first brought to him.)

In March 1943 – two months after the catastrophic German defeat at Stalingrad and amidst increasing anti-Hitler sentiment amongst the army leadership – plotters planted a bomb on Hitler's plane as he flew back to his eastern headquarters from a visit to the Russian front. It was expected to explode in mid-air, but after two hours news came that the plane had landed safely at the Wolf's Lair.

When the plotters recovered the bomb, they discovered that the acid had started to eat through the wire but before the firing pin had been released the acid had frozen. According to one account, Hitler's pilot later explained that he had run into turbulence and, to spare the Führer discomfort, he had taken the plane up to a higher altitude, causing the temperature in the luggage compartment, where the bomb was hidden, to fall sharply and rapidly – and eerily at just the right moment to save Hitler's life again.

A week later, another attempt was made, this time a suicide bomb. Colonel Rudolf von Gerstdorff, an intelligence chief with the army group engaged on the Russian front, was to guide Hitler round an exhibition of war trophies seized during the campaign after the 21 March Heroes' Memorial Day celebration in Berlin. He agreed to blow himself up.

Gerstdorff had a bomb in both pockets of his overcoat. As the Führer moved to the exhibition hall, Gerstdorff primed his bombs by breaking phials of acid which would take 10 minutes to ignite the explosive. In the rush, the plotters had been unable to get shorter fuses.

An aide had promised that Hitler intended to spend at least half an hour there. Unfortunately, Hitler took no interest in the exhibition and showed no inclination to listen to the explanations Gerstdorff wanted to give. He breezed through and was out in just two minutes. Believing his attempt over, Gerstdorff rushed away too, managed to find the toilets empty and disarmed the devices with seconds to spare.

Unbeknown to him, and with huge irony, on leaving the hall Hitler had spotted a captured Soviet tank and spent some time inspecting and clambering over it. It would have provided Gerstdorff with all the time he needed.

As the war spiralled out of control for Germany, and with the D-Day invasion of continental Europe taking hold, the July 1944 bomb plot was one of the most concerted efforts by army officers to eliminate Hitler and secure a negotiated peace. They planned to strike during a military conference at the Führer's Wolf's Lair headquarters in eastern Prussia. Hitler survived in another remarkable turn of fate.

The bomb-laden briefcase brought into the conference room by Count von Stauffenberg was placed under the map table just six feet from Hitler. It rested against the inside of one of the heavy oak supports.

An aide, leaning across to get a better look at the map spread out before the conference, found he was impeded by the briefcase. He casually moved it so it rested on the *outside* of the massive wooden support. That small act saved Hitler's life.

When the bomb exploded less than five minutes later, most of the blast was absorbed by the table support. It was also fortunate for Hitler that he was sitting in front of the main door of the room, which led down a long hallway through which most of the force of the blast escaped.

Hitler suffered only superficial scratches, burst eardrums and a sprained shoulder.

Some other attempts which failed for uncannily unexpected reasons include:

- After the defeat of France, a plot to shoot Hitler while taking the salute at his victory parade in Paris in June 1940 was thwarted when Hitler made his visit four days earlier instead, and stayed just four hours. The parade never took place.
- A suicide effort in November 1943, Operation Overcoat, took advantage of Hitler's known passion for detail and revolved around planning a demonstration of a new uniform to Hitler. A battalion commander volunteered to stash grenades in the pockets of a new overcoat. He would trigger them as Hitler tried on the coat and grapple with the Führer as the four-second fuses took effect. The day before the planned presentation, an Allied air raid on Berlin destroyed the samples, and with that the opportunity disappeared:
- In March 1944 a cavalry captain who agreed to shoot Hitler at a military conference at the Berghof, Hitler's Bavarian retreat, was prevented from entering the meeting room by an SS sentry on the door because the Führer had suddenly ordered that junior ranks should be excluded. His senior officer, unaware of the assassination attempt, actually protested that he needed his aide, but to no avail.

In early 1939, before the outbreak of war, the British military attaché in Berlin, General Sir Noel Mason-MacFarlane, proposed to London that Hitler could be readily assassinated by a sniper, from an apartment building overlooking the Führer's Chancellery. Doing so, he reported, 'could have led to the overthrow of National Socialism and millions of lives could have been saved.' The Government vetoed the idea on the grounds that it was 'unsportsmanlike'.

Britain unknowingly had the secret of the famed German Enigma code 15 years before it realised it. Had it in fact known it had the secret, the entire 1930s, when Nazism rose to spark the Second World War, could well have turned out so differently.

British success in breaking the code that was used by Germany for its military movements was one of the central reasons for the Allied success in World War Two. From as early as the Nazi invasion of Denmark and Norway in April 1940, code breakers at British Intelligence's secret location at Bletchley Park, were reading the secret signals and knew of every major move the enemy planned.

Britain, however, could have broken the system as early as 1924 had they not assumed that the Germans could not be stupid. Since the German armed forces began using the system from the mid-1920s, that capability in the hands of the British authorities could have given the anti-Nazi governments full details of Germany's troop deployments during key crises of the 1930s, many of which hinged on Hitler's brazen bluff. It could have monumentally altered the disastrous appeasement policy that Britain and the Allies followed in response to Hitler's rise to power.

The opportunity to crack the machine two decades earlier came as the machine was first used commercially in Germany in the early 1920s, and the company which made it filed a full patent registration with the London Patent Office in 1924. This described exactly how the machine worked and if British code breakers had followed the wiring pattern set out there they would have had the solution to the military version. But the code breakers could not believe that the military would be so stupid as to use the simple wiring system of a widely available commercial model for the military version. But, astonishingly, that is exactly what the German military did.

When the intelligence services obtained the first military version of Enigma in 1939, they found that the device was wired alphabetically, A to the first contact, B to the second, C to the third and so on. This was the same pattern described in the original commercial patent diagram. It was so obvious that no one ever thought of trying it.

In 2001, when the story emerged from recently released official files, Peter Twinn, the analyst credited with being the first Briton to break an Enigma cipher, reflected, 'I know in retrospect it sounds daft. It was such an obvious thing to do, rather a silly thing, that nobody ever thought it worthwhile trying.'

German arrogance was also a trait that kept Enigma in play. The code-breaking operation came perilously close to being uncovered in August 1943, at the height of the Battle of the Atlantic. The head of the German U-boat forces, Admiral Doenitz, became suspicious that Enigma had been breached after an increase in the number of sinkings of his submarines in remote parts of the Atlantic.

The Abwehr, German Military Intelligence, then received information from Swiss Intelligence, which had an agent in the US Navy Department, telling them expressly that the British had indeed cracked the codes. Although holding an enquiry, the German navy experts concluded that the code was still secure, despite clear evidence to the contrary. It seems they simply could not bring themselves to believe that the complexity behind Enigma could be broken.

The Allies continued to read the code unharassed until the end of the war.

German intelligence missed another opportunity in the spying war in late 1943 when it was presented with a source that provided some of the Allies' topmost secrets. The information was so startlingly good that German spy chiefs ignored it as they suspected it was a trap laid to mislead them.

The star spy was the butler to the British Ambassador to Turkey, then a neutral state but thinking of coming into the war on the Axis side. Elyesa Bazna, codenamed 'Cicero' (after the Roman orator because of his loquaciousness) had access to the careless Ambassador's secret telegram box. He used the Ambassador's regular afternoon piano practice to time his espionage. He always knew while he could hear the music playing in the residence that he was safe rifling the Ambassador's office.

He copied for the Germans papers of astonishing secrecy – records of Churchill's summits with Roosevelt at Casablanca and the three-power summit with Stalin at Teheran that mapped out the grand strategy for victory, plans for the D-Day invasion, including its codename Overlord, and information about bombing raids and the key to the main British cipher.

His German handlers suspected something was not quite right when he claimed not to speak any English, which they later found out was a lie, and that he claimed to work alone, which they later suspected also to be untrue because his description of how he worked which seemed too much for one person to manage. They later spotted his fingers on one photo, which implied he had someone working with him to hold the camera.

The doubts fed German suspicions that they were being set up in an elaborate disinformation scheme. The story they were being given painted a picture of a confident and determined Allied effort, out to fight to the end. This, too, led Germany to believe Britain was trying to hoax them into believing they were stronger than they actually were.

So they discounted the priceless jewels they had in front of them. They showed their mistrust of Bazna, who after six months left the Embassy happy with the payments he thought he had got (his cash turned out to be forged, and worthless).

Had Germany used the information about Allied intentions, their preparedness for D-Day might have been a whole lot better and the outcome very different indeed.

Hitler's curious decision, early in his invasion of the West in May 1940, to halt the rapid advance of his tanks when they had bottled up the bulk of the British Army against the sea at Dunkirk, may have been the moment when Germany began to lose the war. Had he pressed his advantage and crushed the Allied forces, Britain's powers of resistance may have been, like France's, completely neutralised and the war effectively over.

As it was, on 24 May, just a fortnight after German forces had crossed the border into France and the Low Countries, having made breakneck and virtually unhindered progress to the Channel, and with four Panzer divisions at the Aa canal just 12 miles from Dunkirk, Hitler astonishingly ordered his tank commanders to halt the offensive. The decision has mystified military historians to this day.

By the time he relented two days later, the perimeter of Dunkirk had been sufficiently reinforced by the Allies to enable them to resist a further advance. It was too late. In the 'miracle' of Dunkirk that unfolded over the next 11 days, the Allies managed to evacuate 338,000 men to safety. They would go on to the Western Desert later that year and begin the turnaround in North Africa that would bring the war full circle five years later.

Witnesses have given mixed reasons for Hitler's decision, all acute misjudgements. His adjutant said that Hitler believed the British would fight until their ammunition ran out, and then give up, yielding the Nazis a huge prize of prisoners-of-war to be used in peace negotiations.

To his valet, however, Hitler apparently suggested that, 'It is always good to let a broken army return home to show the civilian population what a beating they have had.' To his deputy, Bormann, it was his well-known ambivalence towards England that lay at the heart of his decision. He had purposely let the British escape, but had been disappointed with the reaction, complaining that 'Churchill was quite unable to appreciate the sporting spirit of which I had given proof by refraining from creating an irreparable breach between the British and ourselves.'

Whatever Hitler's true motive, that single calamitous decision, although it would take time to show its full consequence, could well have been the pivotal point of the whole war.

Despite the setback at Dunkirk, Hitler's plans for invading Britain possibly came within a day or so of success. Only another strategic blunder by Goering in the management of the Battle of Britain air campaign allowed the RAF enough time to fend off the assault.

In mid-July 1940, Hitler had ordered Operation Sealion to be launched on 15 September. The air offensive on the RAF bases in southern England was relentlessly maintained for seven weeks through the summer. Losses were running in the range of two fighters for every German plane downed. By 6 September, the RAF was on the point of exhaustion. That day was decisive. Britain had learned, through breaking the German code, that an invasion fleet was massing. Even though the Luftwaffe was receiving crippling damage in the air battles over Kent, a few more days of raiding could have put the remaining air fields out of action and rendered Britain without air cover to defeat the invasion.

On the night of 6 September, however, Goering inexplicably changed the focus of the German attacks from the airfields and aircraft factories to raids on civilian London. That night, 68 bombers attacked the city instead, and the next night the first mass raid took place with over 550 bombers.

The raids would continue for another 57 straight nights, wreaking havoc on the capital. They also gave the RAF a vital reprieve. The growing strength of the air opposition forced Hitler to temporarily postpone the invasion on 17 September. Three weeks later, he cancelled it for good.

How close Britain came to losing its air cover and opening the way for invasion, and all that that might have meant for the collapse of the Allied effort, remains one of the most tantalising 'if onlys' of the Second World War

Two years into the war, and shortly before Pearl Harbor, when Britain fought alone and American isolationism appeared to be as strong as ever, British secret intelligence successfully duped President Roosevelt into committing America to support the war effort against Nazism, using a faked map of the Western Hemisphere that suggested Germany had designs on the United States.

In October 1941, Roosevelt was given the ostensibly German map by his intelligence chief, who was running the forerunner of the CIA. It showed South America reorganised into four mega-states and German bases in central America lying within bombing range of Texas and Florida.

In a national radio address on 27 October, the President disclosed the existence of the map: 'I have in my possession a secret map made in Germany by the planners of the new world order.... The geographical experts of Berlin,' he said to the shocked country, 'have ruthlessly obliterated all the existing boundary lines, bringing the whole continent under their domination....This map makes clear the Nazi design not only against South America but against the United States as well.'

Outrage followed. Sentiment rapidly turned in America. A week later the Senate repealed the Neutrality Act and the House of Representatives, till then an even stronger bastion of isolationism, soon followed. It gave Roosevelt a free hand to conduct covert operations against German submarines in the Atlantic on Britain's side.

The map had worked. It only emerged in the 1960s that it had been a product of a special group of British secret service operatives based in Station M, a forgery factory near Toronto over the border in Canada.

The stunning intelligence coup was overshadowed just 40 days later when America was presented with its very own reason for entering the conflict.

The base at Pearl Harbor missed multiple warnings before the Japanese attack on the morning of 7 December 1941 that could have prevented the full effects of the catastrophe.

The US intelligence agencies had long broken the Japanese military codes, and on 6 December had intercepted 13 parts of a 14-section top-secret message from Tokyo to the Japanese embassy in Washington. The final part was decoded in Washington by 8am on 7 December (2am in Pearl Harbor). It instructed diplomats to present a note to the State Department that lunchtime, rejecting US demands for Japanese withdrawal from China. As soon as Secretary for War General Marshall saw it, he recognised it to be effectively the declaration of war.

However, he would not see it for some hours. His subordinates were under strict instructions not to disturb the General during off-duty hours. It was a Sunday. They therefore waited until after the General's regular morning horse ride and until he had arrived at his command office at mid-morning.

Seeing the meaning of the message, Marshall ordered warnings to be issued to all the bases on the west coast and the Pacific (it was not clear where an attack might strike). They were sent at a minute past noon Washington time (6.01am in Pearl Harbor – still nearly two hours before the first Japanese planes struck).

The messages reached all the bases intended – except Pearl Harbor. Poor atmospheric conditions prevented contact being made, so the warning had to be re-encrypted and sent as a telegram by commercial lines, first to San Francisco and then re-sent by overseas radio on to Honolulu. It did not arrive until 11.45, nearly two hours after the attack had finished. The courier who took the message from the telegraph company's office round to the base apologised to the commander for his own delay, explaining he had taken shelter because of the raid.

Other actions locally that morning proved to be missed opportunities for detecting the attack. At 3.30am, a minesweeper outside the entrance to the harbour spotted and fired on a periscope. (The Japanese deployed a fleet of five midget submarines as part of the raid. At least two managed to penetrate into the harbour.) They reported the incident, but it was not thought significant. So much so that as the minesweeper returned to port, the anti-submarine nets which were drawn open to allow it in were not returned to their action stations, leaving the mouth of the harbour wide open.

Two more midget submarines were spotted at 6.45 and 7am in the vicinity of the harbour mouth. Both were depth-charged and thought to have been blown up.

Lack of coordination of activity reports meant that these suspicious engagements were not seen in conjunction with mysterious radar sightings that were made just after 7am at a tracking station on the tip of Oahu island, 25 miles north of Pearl Harbor. The radar station saw on their screen a vast formation of approaching aircraft about 100 miles north and closing fast. They radioed the sighting to the base, but only two men were on duty there – since breakfast hour had just started – a switchboard operator and one officer. The officer, one Kermit Tyler, a lieutenant in training with the US Army Corps, picked up the phone and told the radar trackers, 'Don't worry about it.' He assumed they were American craft that were due in from the mainland. The radar watchers packed up and went off to breakfast themselves. Nearly an hour's warning was lost.

The complete surprise of the raid increased damage and casualties enormously. There were simply no defensive preparations made. All of the battleships of the Pacific Fleet except one were moored in the harbour. They were all lost or severely damaged – 15 major battleships and cruisers, and three support vessels. 2,403 military personnel and civilians died, and over a thousand more were wounded.

Another small twist of fate, however, worked in America's favour that day. Fortunately for her later prospects in the Pacific theatre, all three of the navy's aircraft carriers were out on manoeuvres. Had they been caught up in the destruction, the future might have turned out very differently. Over the next four years, the aircraft carrier was to emerge as the key to eventual success. Their absence in port that day was the single stroke of good fortune to emerge from the day's appalling run of bad luck.

The fall in February 1942 of Singapore, Britain's pivotal maritime base in southeast Asia, has been described by historians as the most costly and humiliating defeat in Britain's imperial history. It occurred through a series of fiascos in military planning, attitude and organisation, mostly avoidable. The collapse of the 'Gibraltar of the Far East', thought to be impregnable, with such little resistance, spurred the Japanese on, and signalled the historic decline of British power in the region. It was an important step on the path to an independent India, and marked the rise of Japan as a military and economic power.

Astonishingly, at no time did the Japanese enjoy the superiority of numbers. Nor did they have much motor transport – they arrived on cheap bicycles. The attitude of the British authorities did not help either. They doubted Japanese prowess, largely due to a racist attitude against the 'little yellow' nation. According to the British military attaché, 'Our chaps place the Jap somewhere between the Italians and the Afghans.'

When the Japanese arrived from Malaya to the north, Singapore was undefended – all the guns pointed seawards; no one had anticipated an invasion from the other direction. According to author Philip Knightley's account, the secretary of the golf club had refused to allow guns to be placed on his greens until his committee had been consulted, and last-minute defences were delayed for over a week in a dispute over local coolies' wages. As bombs dropped on the city, street lights stayed on because no one could find the key to the master switch to turn them out. The Post Office even cut off phone calls to the front once the wartime regulation three minutes were up.

The Japanese overran the 'fortress' island in just six days, capturing 85,000 Allied troops as prisoners of war. In his diary, the Japanese commander Tomoyuki Yamashita wrote, 'My attack on Singapore was a bluff. I had 30,000 men and was outnumbered more than three to one....I was extremely frightened that the British would discover our numerical weakness and lack of supplies and force me into disastrous street fighting. But they never did. My bluff worked.'

One of the earliest signs that Hitler suspected he was losing the war came a year after his invasion of Russia – by a trick using cigar smoke. He paid a surprise visit to the Finnish leader, Marshal Carl Mannerheim, who was also engaged against the Soviet army, in June 1942.

The visit was ostensibly to mark the Marshal's 75th birthday. They met in a cramped railway carriage on the Finnish-Soviet front. It was intended to be symbolic of the mutual strength of the Allies, but Mannerheim discovered a deeper truth when he lit up a cigar in the Führer's presence. Hitler was renowned for his abhorrence of smoking. Mannerheim is said to have deliberately blown the smoke into Hitler's face. While adjutants froze expecting a reaction, Hitler meekly showed none.

Mannerheim deduced that the war was going badly for Germany. Had Hitler shown any reaction, it would have been a sign of strength. By not batting an eyelid, Hitler gave away his weakness. He needed the Finns to keep their efforts up. He could not afford to antagonise their leader.

At the end of the meeting, Mannerheim was certain of the outcome of the Nazi-Soviet conflict.

The entire secret plan for the D-Day invasion of Normandy was lost by a British Intelligence officer only two months before the operation was set to go. It contained every detail of the radio wavelengths and codes to be used by the forces involved. It also revealed the layout and strengths of the assault formations and clues to the date.

The officer, a deputy to Brigadier Lionel Harris, chief of the telecommunications branch of the Supreme Allied Headquarters, had somehow lost the bulky document while travelling home through London's Waterloo station in April 1944. Harris suspected him of after-hours drinking. Unless planners were going to take a huge gamble, the breach of security would mean the abandonment of the operation that had been in preparation for nearly two years.

Just as Harris was about to pass on the news to his senior, he received a phone call from the Lost Property Office of Scotland Yard, the capital's police headquarters, reporting that a briefcase had been found with some papers that appeared to be concerned with wireless. According to one account, there was also a bottle of beer in the case as well. The police officer wanted to know whether the documents were important, and if so, could someone come round to collect them as he was short-staffed and could not spare anyone to deliver them.

Harris himself dashed round to retrieve the plans. He found out that they had been handed in by a taxi driver, who had discovered the briefcase in the back of his cab after dropping off a somewhat worse-for-wear passenger at Waterloo station.

British authorities were able to keep well informed of German troop movements across the Channel through one of the most outlandishly simple ruses. They had French intelligence operatives set themselves up as laundrymen. Having established a reputation for low prices and good service, they had secured business from most of the German divisions in the Channel coast region.

Bizarrely, when the German units moved on, they showed a religious zeal for collecting their laundry, even leaving a forwarding address for the items that were not ready. As one account puts it, the German army 'might be going to Valhalla, but they were not prepared to go without their linen.'

This surveillance revealed that shortly before D-Day, the SS's panzer divisions based elsewhere in France and between Antwerp and Brussels had not moved, indicating that they were still being misled by the Allied deception plan which was misdirecting the Germans to expect the invasion further east near Calais.

The choice of date for launching D-Day rested heavily on the accuracy of three two-man weather forecasting teams, from the British Meteorological Office, the Royal Navy and the US military.

The original date, 5 June 1944, was postponed at just two days' notice because the two British teams forecast poor weather. The Americans disagreed, and even tried to force the British forecasters to change their prediction. The Brits stuck firm, wisely as it turned out – the 5th saw Force 6 winds and high seas.

The planners were on a knife-edge. If they could not go on the following day, 6 June, the invasion would have to be put back until 19 June, the next time the tides would be right. Fortunately, on 4 June a break in the weather convinced the forecasters that the conditions for 6 June would be favourable. They gave the go-ahead. D-Day dawned with perfect weather and little swell.

Few realised at the time how close the call actually was. Lawrence Hogben, one of only two of the forecasters left alive, recalled in 2004, that if they had been less confident and elected to delay until the 19th, the outcome of the invasion would have been an 'utter catastrophe'.

'As it happened, on the 17th, all six of us produced a forecast for the 19th for almost perfect conditions, so they would definitely have gone ahead.' In fact, the 19th saw the biggest storm of the century come up the Channel. 'If they'd landed that day, I doubt many landing craft would have even made it to the beaches. It doesn't bear thinking about.'

The British and Canadian landing beaches for D-Day were all originally to be named after fish – Gold, Sword and Jelly. The last name, however, ran foul of a 1943 edict from Churchill which had laid down for the first time general rules for naming military operations. It specified that those in which large numbers of men were expected to lose their lives should not be named with 'a boastful or over-confident sentiment' or be 'of a frivolous character.'

It was quickly realised that 'Jelly' would not suffice, and it became Juno, which, according to one account, was the name of the wife of one of the Canadian planners.

The collapsing the German war effort after D-Day should have ended in the complete destruction of Paris as Nazi forces evacuated eastwards. The city was saved because the signals clerk on duty the night the order arrived from Berlin to blow up the city was an enthusiastic Francophile art lover. He sat on the instruction until it was too late to implement it.

On the evening of 22 August, with the Allies still two days away from Paris, Hitler sent a telegram to the commander in the city instructing that 'Paris must only fall into the hands of the enemy as a field of rubble.' Explosives experts had been feverishly working for days to put in place explosive charges to destroy all 45 of the city's bridges, the Eiffel Tower, the Elysee Palace and several industrial targets. As well as destroying the buildings, the explosions were designed to create a firestorm that would destroy the historic heart of Paris.

The signals officer on duty that night at the German headquarters who received the telegram happened to be 26-year-old Ernst von Bressendorf, whose artistic passions made him recoil at the vandalism of the order. Aware of how close the Allies were, and that the war was effectively lost, but also that direct disobedience would lead to his execution, he delayed passing the telegram up to his commanding officer (who, as a strict Prussian, was known for unquestioningly obeying orders).

By the time he did so, his commanding officer, General Dietrich von Choltitz, had also become convinced of the futility of the act. Paris was saved. On 25 August, when the Allies arrived, they found it intact.

After the war, von Bressendorf worked on the reconciliation of French and German families. He became revered in France as the man who saved Paris. His dearest wish was to live until the 50th anniversary of the liberation in 1994, and had been invited to the celebrations. He died on 19 August, six days short of the anniversary.

The Leaning Tower of Pisa came within two hours of being blown up by advancing American troops in July 1944, according to a veteran of the Fifth Army speaking for the first time in 1999.

Sergeant Leon Weckstein had been ordered by his commander to deploy a detachment to scout the tower which was thought to be occupied by German observers at the top to direct artillery fire on to the American forces.

His commander, Colonel James Woods, had told him, 'If you see any Germans up the tower, we'll have to demolish it. We are losing too many men.' Weckstein spent as long as he could on the mission to avoid reporting back. 'I thought I saw German rifles and helmets through the pillars around the top of the tower, but I couldn't be absolutely sure. So I hesitated.'

He later reported back that there were no Germans visible, and after two tense hours during which the tower was one radio message away from being obliterated, Weckstein was recalled. 'The attack on the Leaning Tower was called off.'

The impetus towards the world's first atomic attack, on Hiroshima in August 1945, may have been unduly spurred on by a translator's interpretation of a single word in a Japanese press statement.

At the end of the Big Three conference at Potsdam at the end of July, Allied leaders issued a declaration demanding the unconditional surrender of Japan. Japan, which had begun to put out feelers for a negotiated peace, and hoping to continue the nascent diplomatic contacts, replied with a holding statement to the world's press that intended to offer 'no comment' on the unconditional surrender demand.

The Japanese word used – *mokusatsu* – has several shades of meaning: to ignore, to refrain from comment or even, in some contexts, to seek more information. The American interpreter who provided the translation for Secretary of War Stimson, who was advising President Truman on plans to use the atomic bomb, used 'ignore'. The Americans stiffened their attitude towards Japan's apparent intransigence, and quickened the preparations for the drop on Hiroshima. Had a different slant been used, the moral pressure not to inflict the terrifying weapon on civilians might have been too strong to resist.

The Nazi attempt to build an atomic bomb was the nightmare dread of Allied governments during the Second World War. Evidence after the war showed that German scientists' early research had put them ahead of the Americans by the end of 1941. They had two Nobel Prize winners working on the programme – the co-discover of nuclear fission, Otto Hahn, and Werner Heisenberg who, by as early as 1942, understood what was needed to build an atomic device.

But it was the German assessment of how long the war would last – an assumed maximum of 18 months – that drove them to relegate the atom bomb low down their list of priorities, behind the V1 and V2 rocket programmes, and the development of the jet engine. They did not put effort into the bomb simply because they judged it would take longer to develop than the war would last.

By the time it dawned on Germany military leaders that the war would drag on, shortage of materials and damage from Allied air raids made it impossible to restart the programme. The chance was lost.

Ironically, it was the threat of a German bomb that gave impetus to the American Manhattan Project. Einstein, who had left Nazi Germany for America only because of Hitler's anti-Semitic policies, wrote two letters to President Roosevelt in 1939 and 1940 detailing the advances Germany was making and urging him to commit vast resources of manpower and money. Roosevelt obliged.

When the German scientists heard of the American effort, they estimated that from where they had left off, had they applied the same effort, they might have secured a working bomb in late 1944 or early 1945 – six months before the Americans.

If only, at the right time, there had been a German advocate to write a letter to Hitler…

Nagasaki, destroyed in 1945 by the second nuclear bomb to be dropped on Japan, only became the target after the first choice city was found on the morning of the attack to be covered by cloud.

The 210,000 citizens of Kokura, about 100 miles southwest of Hiroshima which had been devastated three days before, should have been vaporised on 9 August. It was selected for having the largest ammunition factory in western Japan. The complex, where 12,000 people worked, was the aiming point for the bomb.

The B-29 bomber was overhead by 10am and circled the city three times with its bomb door open, but cloud as well as smoke from an air raid the day before obscured the ground. So it gave up and flew on to Nagasaki, an hour further south. At 11.02am it dropped the device there. Some 74,000 people died immediately, and as many again would die later from the longer-term effects.

On the 60th anniversary in 2005, Kokura mounted an exhibition to commemorate its narrow escape. It ran under the tile, 'That day: if it had been clear…'

Japan's plans for its own terror weapon – balloons carrying plague and other deadly diseases across the Pacific to the United States – never came to fruition because of fears by Japanese commanders that they might blow back on to home territory.

The story only emerged in 1987. In late 1944, as the war closed in on Japan, scientists at the notorious biological warfare unit, Unit 731, developed a paper balloon capable of carrying a very small bomb. The plans were for the devices to spread plague, anthrax, typhus and other diseases across the United States.

A trial attempt between November 1944 and January 1945 sent over 9,000 of the balloons towards the American continent carrying incendiary devices. Only 10 per cent of them reached their destination. Few did any damage. Five children and an adult were killed by one in Oregon (the only casualties from hostile action on American soil), and several forest fires were started in the west coast states. They were recorded as landing over a wide area of Alaska and Canada, and some are believed to have travelled as far as Chicago.

Although unsatisfactory as a bombing mission, the numbers which did make it to America would have been more than enough to cause a catastrophe had they carried biological agents. Ironically, it was that risk that also scuppered the project. Japanese regional commanders feared that unhelpful winds could send some of the lethal weapons off track and back into Japan. No plague bombs were ever despatched. But the winter of 1944 to 1945 had shown how close the American heartland had come to devastation.

One of the war's most wanted individuals, Josef Mengele, the doctor responsible for performing medical experiments on concentration camp inmates at Auschwitz, miraculously evaded detection by Allied authorities – because of his lifelong vanity.

In June 1945, a month after the end of the war, Mengele had been detained by American forces along with thousands of other Germans and interred in a holding camp in Bavaria. He even registered under his real name. He escaped notice, however, because he could not be readily identified as a member of the SS. When he had joined the elite force in 1938, he had refused to have his blood group tattooed on his chest or arm as was normally required for an entrant. He persuaded his seniors that, as a doctor, he could look after himself. The real reason, according to his wife, was that he was so self-obsessed about his looks and particularly the smoothness of his skin – he used to stand in front of a full-length mirror admiring its perfection – that he did not want it blemished in any way.

The absence of the telltale insignia that all American troops had been told to look out for literally saved his skin. The Americans unknowingly released Mengele in September.

Mengele had no idea how lucky he had been. Two months before his capture, he had been formally declared a war criminal. The information failed to percolate down to the confused transit camps in time to catch him.

He managed to fade into civilian life in post-war Germany for four years and then he quietly slipped away to Argentina in 1949. He was able to live out another 30 years in various South American hideaways until he died while swimming in Brazil in February 1979, a fact that did not become public until 1992.

A bridge across a river in southern Hungary was discovered in October 1999 to still be rigged with dynamite dating back to the end of the Second World War. The village of Holloshaza was the scene of heavy fighting as the invading Soviet Army fought its way to Budapest. The retreating Germans had planned to blow up the bridge but fled, leaving the explosives in place. The bridge then enjoyed 55 years of traffic usage before someone spotted the wires.

The Korean War of 1950–53 was the first military conflict of the Cold War. It remains technically unresolved to this day. Bizarrely, it might have been the United States that unwittingly prompted the North Koreans to invade the South in June 1950.

Dean Acheson, the Secretary of State, delivered a speech in January that year defining American security interests in the East Asian sphere. He appeared to be precise: 'Our defensive perimeter runs from the Aleutians [off Alaska] to Japan, the Ryukyus [Okinawa] and down to the Philippines...So far as the military security of other areas in the Pacific is concerned, it must be clear that no person can guarantee theses areas against military attack.'

His description excluded the Korean peninsula, and all American forces had just been withdrawn the previous year. Historians dispute whether the speech was more forceful in encouraging the North to go ahead with its assault, or in motivating the South's leaders, now feeling exposed to the Communist threat, to force the issue so as to inveigle the US back into providing defence support.

Either way, five months after Acheson's remarks, the Koreas were at war, with the US and Chinese troops soon to follow.

There were echoes of this carelessness in the lead up to the 1990 invasion of Kuwait by Iraq's Saddam Hussein. As Iraqi pressure on Kuwait grew in July that year, the American ambassador in Baghdad, April Glaspie, was summoned at short notice to an audience with Saddam. Not having time to consult Washington for specific guidance, she followed a general conciliatory line trying to defuse the growing fears in Baghdad of the US taking sides.

She told Saddam that the US had 'no opinion on inter-Arab disputes such as your border dispute with Kuwait.' While also reiterating that the US could never excuse settlement of disputes by any but peaceful means, she could not back up this view with a threat to intervene by the US in the event of hostilities as she had no authority from Washington to do so.

It seems that Saddam probably interpreted this message as a signal that the US would not intervene. Eight days later, he invaded Kuwait.

The Cuban missile crisis in 1962 at the height of the Cold War is acknowledged by historians to have been the closest the world has come to nuclear war. As the tense stand-off developed – on 22 October, Day 8 of the crisis, the United States had moved its forces up to the third highest level of readiness, and had nuclear-armed B-52s in the skies ready to launch attacks on the Soviet Union – any misjudgement was potentially catastrophic.

It was revealed only 30 years later that on that day over the Kamchatka peninsula in Siberia, a B-52 strayed into Soviet airspace. Two MIG-17 fighters were sent up with orders to destroy it. General Boris Surikov, a Defence Ministry official, recalled how the encounter was tracked on screens in Moscow. 'I could see two green dots – the MIGs – and one red dot – the B-52 – steadily converging. No one…doubted that if the red dot disappeared off the screen, then it would be the beginning of an atomic war. When the dots were only about 50km [30 miles] apart, the two green ones suddenly reversed course.'

It turned out that they did not have sufficient fuel left. On the likely assumption that they were flying close to their maximum speed of 715mph, they had been just two and a half minutes from their target.

In 2002, an even closer episode was revealed, when the actions of a single Soviet officer appear to have prevented accidental nuclear war breaking out. On 27 October 1962, the day before the Soviet leadership finally agreed the deal to withdraw its missiles from Cuba, tensions were rising to their highest crescendo. Satellite reconnaissance of Cuba showed the nuclear missiles installed there had become fully operational and hours earlier an American U2 spy plane had been shot down over Siberia.

Off Cuba, a US navy ship, the *USS Beale*, had encountered a Soviet submarine and launched an attack with depth charges. It was unaware that the submarine was armed with a nuclear torpedo. On board, the Soviet crew believed war had broken out and started the procedure for firing its own nuclear device. It was authorised to do so without orders from Moscow on the approval of its three officers.

According to the account, disclosed for the first time by a sailor who had witnessed the chaos in the submarine, the captain Valentin Savitsky and another officer decided in favour of launching. The third, Vasily Arkhipov, refused. His single-handed action calmed Savitsky, persuaded him to surface and defused the crisis.

At the very moment this was happening at sea, Kennedy and Khrushchev were striking the deal which ended the stand-off. The settlement was announced the very next morning.

In the American homeland, there were also several near misses that could have triggered catastrophe in the heightened atmosphere of panic. On 26 October 1962, a routine test firing of an intercontinental ballistic missile went ahead at Vandenberg military air base in California despite the crisis being close to its gravest point. No one had thought to stand down the test in the circumstances. Although unarmed, the base was on the second highest state of alert, and all other standby missiles had been nuclear-armed in readiness. Had the Soviet Union detected the launch, it might well have concluded that America had decided to commence a first strike.

At an air force base in Montana, the new Minuteman missile was about to be commissioned into service when the crisis broke. They were rushed into operation, with several safety checks bypassed. Crews were also deployed before they had completed their training and certified as being competent to manage the launch process.

The strangest incident occurred on the night of 25 October when a sentry on duty at a base near Duluth, Minnesota, spotted and fired at an intruder trying to climb the perimeter fence. The alarm was raised throughout the base and, under a synchronisation arrangement, across all the bases in the surrounding region. However, at Volk Field, Wisconsin, the wrong signal sounded – the alarm indicating the nuclear war had actually started. Pilots had been told that there would be no drills during the present crisis, so they responded as they were trained to do. They were taxiing their fully-primed nuclear-armed planes down the runway before the base commander, who had the presence of mind to ring Duluth, cancelled the alert. He had to send his staff car into the middle of the runway and flash its lights to abort the take-offs.

The day of the *Beale* incident recounted above – the darkest day of the crisis – had already seen a bizarre close shave that morning caused by a routine drill conducted at an advance warning radar station at Moorestown, New Jersey. A test tape was run which simulated a missile attack from the Caribbean. In a potentially fatal coincidence, at the same moment what was later identified as a friendly US spy satellite was detected on its normal flight path over Cuba. It appeared in exactly the same place and at exactly the same time as the test simulation of an enemy missile. When the test finished, the object was still there. According to the station log of the incident, operators 'became confused' about what was real and what was part of the drill. They notified central command that America was under attack from Cuba and that the apparent missile was targeted on Tampa, Florida, with impact in two minutes.

The Situation Room dealing with the Missile Crisis was notified that war had started. When nothing happened two minutes later, the station began to realise its mistake. Other tracking stations began to confirm the true identity of the mystery object. Ironically, and fortunately, on this occasion there simply had not been enough time for the military high command to make a decision to respond.

In 1985, during evidence to an Australian Commission of Inquiry on nuclear weapons tests in the 1950s, it was revealed that British Ministry of Defence scientists considered using Duncansby Head near Wick in northeast Scotland as the site for Britain's nuclear bomb tests. It was eventually ruled out – only on the grounds that weather records showed it rained too much for the monitoring equipment. The tests were transferred to the remote Australian outback.

The inquiry heard evidence that in 1953 the government also inspected potential sites at Skipsea on the Yorkshire coast and Mablethorpe in Lincolnshire. They were ruled out because of the likelihood of 'very considerable local feeling'.

One of the most alarming periods in the Cold War for America – the so-called 'bomber gap' in the mid-1950s which diverted a billion dollars of defence expenditure to the problem of catching up with the Soviets – was an entirely nonexistent threat created by a simple Kremlin ruse to fool the United States.

The appearance of a new long-range nuclear bomber, the M-4 Bison, at the Soviet Union's annual May Day parade in Red Square in 1954, was viewed at the time as not particularly significant as the craft looked like a prototype that would not be ready until at least

1960. Alarm bells were set ringing in Washington 14 months later when the American military attaché was invited to a celebration in July 1955 of Red Air Force Day. A display put on at Moscow's Tushino airport astonished the diplomat as there seemed to be far more of the craft than America had thought.

He sent alarmed messages back to the Pentagon and the CIA, which led them to make an urgent revision of assumptions about Soviet strategy. Whereas the Americans were focusing on a missile strategy, the Soviets appeared to be focusing on the long-range bomber to deliver nuclear weapons. And America was woefully behind in that category of weapon.

The revised estimate was leaked to the press, leading to a Senate inquiry. The Eisenhower administration had to come up with another $928 million to buy far more B-52 bombers than expected.

In fact, the attaché at Tushino had been cleverly, but simply, duped. The flypast of the Bisons had been multiples of the same small number of craft, circling out of sight of the viewing stand and repeating their runs over and over again, to give the impression of a larger fleet than actually existed.

It cost the Americans a billion dollars, but in the end the ruse backfired on the Soviets as it left the United States far more powerful in the air than they ever intended to be. By the late 1950s, spy planes had revealed the silos that showed that in fact the real Soviet strength lay in intercontinental missiles.

An even more surreal dimension to the bomber threat emerged in 1994 when the deputy head of Russia's strategic air force revealed that throughout the Cold War, for safety reasons, the Soviet air force planes never flew with genuine nuclear weapons but were loaded only with imitations.

Exploding the myth of the threat of air-dropped bombs, Anatoli Solovyov wrote in a Russian newspaper article that ground staff practised loading real weapons, but for flights always replaced them with dummies. It was 'a reasonable decision not to expose ourselves and others to excessive risks.'

America and Britain both missed an opportunity to acquire the secrets of the Soviet nuclear missile programme early on in the Cold War. It would have been an intelligence coup that would have altered the course of the superpower struggle. But staff at both embassies in Moscow failed to follow up on the offer.

The story only emerged from the Russian security service archives in 2001. Alexander Orlov, a 27-year-old junior member of a secret research team, approached the American embassy shortly after the Soviet Union had successfully conducted its first nuclear explosion in August 1949. He was offering a copy of the entire Soviet missile programme for the next 15 years. America's normal intelligence-gathering method relied on remote listening stations to monitor missile tests and deduce the state of progress from data on flight trials. They were now being offered the full technical blueprint, which included plans for intercontinental missiles and possibly satellite development and launches.

He tried to attract attention by lurking outside the embassy. He even threw a note through the half-open window of an embassy car offering to sell the material, but no one at the embassy ever responded. He then tried the British embassy, slipping inside the compound one night in September 1950. But there is no record of any meeting or incident report. Four days afterwards, he was picked up by the KGB. He was executed a year later, officially for treason and espionage on behalf of the British secret service.

At the time, the West knew next to nothing about Soviet intentions and capabilities, which adds to the mystery why the astonishing opportunity presented by Alexander Orlov went begging.

The West's frontline defences in Europe against Soviet ground attack in the Cold War might have rested on chickens had a plan developed by British nuclear scientists been accepted.

The Blue Peacock tactical nuclear mine project was designed to stall an enemy surge across Germany. The seven-tonne bombs, carrying half the power of the weapon that destroyed Nagasaki, would be deployed at strategic points when an invasion was judged imminent. Production of the first 10 mines was ordered in July 1957. The problem was how to keep the inside of the bomb warm enough for it to work in winter. Planners proposed to fill the weapons with live chickens, with enough food and water for one week, the expected maximum lifetime of the weapon. Their body temperature would provide the required heat for the device to stay operational.

The scheme was never put into practice. The Ministry of Defence cancelled the project in February 1958.

On 20 February 1971, a technician at the United States' emergency broadcasting system designed to issue national warnings of impending nuclear attack inadvertently sent out a test message under the password signifying it to be a genuine alert. Over 2,500 radio and television stations received the message. It told them to close down broadcasting and instruct listeners to await a broadcast by the president.

The mistake was not noticed for 26 minutes. Even then, the correction message was sent without the genuine password. It would be 40 minutes before a message with the correct password, signifying the alert to be a false alarm, was issued.

Fortunately, no action was taken by anyone on the receiving end of the message. In fact, it was ignored by a large number of stations and most of the American population. Press reports described a comedy of errors. Many stations did not look at their teletype printers until hours after the message was sent so carried on heedless of the apparent emergency. Others listened to their neighbouring stations to see who would sign off first. The correspondent of the London *Times* reported, 'One or two went off

111

the air but did not have the heart to tell their listeners that world war was about to break out.'

For some listeners, it was reminiscent of the 1938 *War of the Worlds* broadcast that had created nationwide panic amongst listeners. Not on this occasion. All of which made the day's events an even more alarming outcome for the Pentagon's civil defence planners. An official at the Civil Defence Office reflected that whether people would respond to such alerts was 'one of the things I've always wondered.' Now they knew.

Britain's nuclear readiness has sometimes been little more reassuring. One episode uncovered by Whitehall-watcher Peter Hennessy in 1999 recalled a critical moment on 25 June 1963, when, had the Soviet Union wanted to launch an attack, British warning systems would never have known about it.

It came during the crucial last day of the Lord's Test against the West Indies when the match was on a knife-edge in the final over. Colin Cowdrey, left arm encased in plaster from an earlier injury, had to return to the crease with two balls of the match left, England needing six to win, and their opponents one wicket for victory.

At that moment, every single screen of the Ballistic Missile Early Warning system was showing the live broadcast of the cricket from the BBC.

Another alarming incident took place in November 1979 when President Carter's National Security Adviser, Zbigniew Brzezinski, received a middle-of-the-night phone call from his deputy, Colonel William Odom, reporting that the country's early warning systems were indicating that the Soviet Union had just launched 220 intercontinental missiles at the United States.

Shortly after, Odom rang again to confirm the bad news and to add that the correct figure was 2,200 missiles – the dreaded all-out nuclear attack. Just before he was about to call Carter, who would have had between three and seven minutes to make a decision, Odom telephoned a third time to tell him it was all a mistake. A technician had loaded an exercise tape used for simulating war games into the computer system.

The closest the world has come to accidental war seems to have been in 1983 as the stability of the Soviet Union was starting to unravel. In a period which saw a change of leadership three times in 30 months after the death of Leonid Brezhnev, the last Communist strongman, the Soviet leadership was intensely fearful of the apparent solidity of the Western bloc, now concertedly led by Ronald Reagan and Margaret Thatcher.

As the new Soviet head, Yuri Andropov, struggled to assume leadership, Reagan had made his 'evil empire' speech and then, in March 1983, announced his 'Star Wars' strategic defence initiative aiming to equip America with the power to shoot down incoming missiles while still in space. When Soviet jets shot down a Korean airliner which had strayed into Siberian airspace in September, the tensions only heightened.

The Soviets were also aware of a major NATO military exercise planned for early November to test command coordination procedures for activating nuclear war. In the febrile atmosphere, there was a growing fear of this exercise being a mask for an actual attack. A sudden flurry of communications traffic between Britain and America in late October seriously raised suspicions in Moscow's mind.

In fact, the flood of messages represented anything but increased collaboration. The exchanges were in response to Britain's outrage at the US invasion of the Caribbean (and Commonwealth) island of Grenada on 25 October of which the British government had not been informed in advance. The Soviet analysts, able only to detect the scale but not the content of the traffic, had no reason to suspect the sudden change was due to the two powers arguing furiously with each other. It seemed instead to be confirming greater consultation between their biggest enemies.

As the exercise got under way, on the night of 8/9 November, the KGB despatched only the second 'flash' signal ever sent throughout the Cold War (the other was during the Cuban Missile Crisis) to all Soviet stations in Europe warning that American bases had been put on alert. It was incorrect, but for two days until the NATO exercise ended as planned on 11 November, the Soviet Union was poised to unleash its arsenal at any sign of further threat.

Unknowingly, the world teetered on the brink for 48 hours.

We must all hope that BBC Radio's flagship morning news programme *Today* does not suffer a long-running strike. It was revealed in 2002 that part of Britain's nuclear strike orders for the Royal Navy's Trident submarine force includes authorising the captain to begin nuclear action if the submarine is unable to pick up the programme for a secret number of consecutive days. Security officials were reported to believe that failure to detect the programme would be a reliable sign that Britain had suffered a catastrophic nuclear attack.

In March 2001, a former CIA operative disclosed that an Agency deception campaign in the 1960s that backfired, had probably been responsible for the modern development of chemical and biological weapons.

Raymond Garthoff revealed that the FBI and the US Army began a campaign in the mid-1960s to convince the Soviet Union that the US had developed chemical and biological weapons of mass destruction. The Pentagon had actually determined that the whole concept was a blind alley and that feasible armaments were not possible. The plan, then, was to trick the Communists into wasting billions of scarce roubles finding out the same (much like the

Soviet 'bomber gap' ruse had done to the Americans, although they did not know it at the time).

The plot backfired when the Soviets succeeded where the US had not, and within a few years lethal drug-resistant strains of smallpox and anthrax and new nerve gases were in the Soviet armoury.

The irony deepened when, with the collapse of the Soviet Union, the trained experts and stocks of weapons-grade germs became highly vulnerable to offers from outside the country. Proliferation to rogue states, the nightmare of the first decade of the 21st century, thus conceivably traces itself directly back to America's clever idea half a century ago.

Live anthrax weapons lay undisturbed in a Norwegian museum for 60 years before they were tested and neutralised. They were part of one of the world's earliest, and more bizarre, biological warfare attacks dating from the First World War.

A Swedish mercenary, Baron Otto von Rosen, was sent by the German secret service in the winter of 1917 to sabotage British Arctic supply lines to Russia. He was armed with 19 disease-laden sugar cubes which he was to feed to horses and reindeer being used to pull supply sledges from ports in northern Norway across the top of Scandinavia into Russia.

He was captured, and two of the cubes were put on display in the police museum in Trondheim. They lay there until 1997 when a concerned official sent them to a British biological warfare laboratory for testing. The spores were found still to be very much alive.

A week-long war was fought between neighbouring El Salvador and Honduras in July 1969 after one had beaten the other at football.

The so-called 'Soccer War' was sparked when El Salvador had beaten Honduras 3–0 in a World Cup qualifying match in San

Salvador. The match, a return leg after Honduras had won the first game 1–0, was played in an atmosphere of intense rivalry. During the anthem-playing ceremony at the start of the game, instead of the Honduran flag – which had already been burned in front of the spectators – the hosts ran up the flagpole a dirty, tattered dish rag.

After the victory, riots broke out back in Honduras against the 300,000 Salvadoreans who had migrated there for work. A large number were forced to flee home. As tension continued to increase, El Salvador invaded Honduras and 6,000 people were killed or wounded in the conflict before a ceasefire was brokered.

It was not the first time that two Latin American countries had descended into war from trivial beginnings. In 1932, a postage stamp printed by Paraguay prompted neighbouring Bolivia to invade. The stamp portrayed a map of the region with the large disputed border area of Chaco marked as belonging to Paraguay. To add insult, a slogan was added asserting 'Has been, is and will be.'

Bolivia attacked, won initial success and then collapsed. In the ensuing three-year war, Paraguay won most of the territory by the time hostilities ceased. In the peace treaty which followed in 1938, Paraguay gained three-quarters of the disputed area. A hundred thousand people died in the conflict.

5

Science – Inspiration, Invention and Intrigue

William Herschel, who in 1781 became the first person in history to discover a planet of the solar system, might have had it named after him had it not been for the overenthusiasm of King George III and Herschel's enforced riposte.

The King awarded the German-born émigré a pension on news of the discovery. Herschel felt obliged to reciprocate and declared the name of the new planet to be Georgium Sidus in the royal honour. This naturally irked non-British astronomers, even leading a few to start calling the planet 'Herschel' instead. For 40 years, it wavered between the two.

In the end, the cheek of trying to label a planet after a British Royal proved too much for continental astronomers and some years after Herschel's death in 1822 the alternative idea of Johann Bode, who had confirmed the discovery in 1781, prevailed. He had proposed Uranus, from the mythological thread connecting the previously outermost planet, Saturn (father of Jupiter). So the next planet out should be Uranus, father of Saturn.

Eli Whitney's invention of the cotton gin in 1793 revolutionised the cotton-growing industry by cracking the biggest obstacle to mass production – how to separate the cotton fibre from the seeds. Hand processing made cotton extremely expensive and difficult to produce, but the dexterity required to separate the materials looked impossible to recreate mechanically.

It was solved in a flash of observation. Whitney was inspired by watching a cat clawing a dead chicken and getting only the feathers. Cheap to make, the cotton gin – a revolving cylinder of nails that was turned to draw the cotton through small slotted holes – enabled a single operator to make 50 pounds of cotton a day instead of one.

Pioneer tunnel engineer, Marc Isambard Brunel, father of Isambard Kingdom Brunel, invented the first mechanical borer for tunnelling under river beds in 1818 after watching how the shipworm, a notorious wood-boring mollusc, was able to eat its way through ships' hulls while protecting its head from the pressure of the material collapsing around it.

He designed an ingenious iron-framed device which protected workers from cave-ins as they cut through unstable sea beds, and used it to build the first underwater tunnel in the world, the Thames Tunnel, between Rotherhithe and Wapping which took 18 years to complete between 1825 and 1843. It is still used to this day.

The stethoscope was invented in 1816 by French doctor René Laennec because his patient was young, female and on the plump side.

Laennec suspected the woman to be suffering from a heart problem. He felt awkward adopting the usual method of examination – holding his ear close to the woman's naked chest. Her 'great degree' of fatness also hampered the alternative of holding his hand to her chest. He improvised by using a rolled up newspaper, and was astonished at the amplification effect it produced.

He later developed a 12-inch-long wooden tube, and had invented the stethoscope.

Walter Hunt, a New York mechanic, invented the safety pin in 1849 in just three hours, to pay off a $15 debt. He saw no commercial value in the idea, agreed to sell all his rights to it for $400 to the friend he was in debt to, and felt pleased to have made a $385 profit on the deal.

The friend, and future manufacturers, subsequently reaped millions from the device.

The development of the railways in Britain in the 1820s and 1830s might not have progressed as rapidly as it did if George Stephenson had not deliberately lied to parliament.

After the inauguration of Stephenson's first railway, the Stockton–Darlington line in 1825, a rush of other proposals were put forward for other routes. A parliamentary committee scrutinised Stephenson closely on this newfangled form of transport. The chief concern was speed, and the fear that too rapid speeds would cause physical or mental injury to passengers.

Stephenson lied when he told the committee that no engine would ever be able to travel faster than 12mph. He knew it was already possible to reach at least double that speed.

Had he been honest, he would have reinforced parliament's fears, and the prospects for rapid expansion of the railway network, which was to bring untold economic and social change to Britain in the next 30 years, might well have been significantly checked.

Thomas Edison, inventor of electric lighting, also used outright deception to advance his cause. Without it, he would not have secured the funds necessary to develop his ideas to commercial levels.

In 1878 he had approached New York bankers J.P. Morgan for $50,000 to equip the laboratory he needed to make a marketable electric light. If it were feasible, it would make a fortune for investors. But few believed it possible. The bank failed to sell the shares in the company they set up, so Edison lied to New York newspaper reporters that he had already invented the device. It tipped the balance, the shares were snapped up and Edison got his $50,000.

It would take him a year, working 20 hours a day, to develop the world's first working electric light. He did indeed make a fortune for everyone involved. But without the lie, he might never have had the chance, and we might never have had the light bulb.

Charles Goodyear's discovery in 1839, after five years of fruitless experimenting on how to make rubber in a usable and durable form, came after he tried to cover up his work from his long-suffering wife. He was trying out another new idea mixing sulphur with rubber when Clarissa returned home unexpectedly. According to one account, as the couple were by now nearing penury he had promised her that he would cease his apparently pointless tinkering with rubber and get a proper job. When he heard her arriving home, he stuffed the materials into the family oven to hide them from her.

He later returned to the kitchen to retrieve them, and discovered that the heat of the oven had changed the properties of the rubber. It was the clue he was looking for. He had discovered the principle of vulcanisation, which made natural rubber resistant to temperature change (unvulcanised rubber melted in heat and became brittle when cold), and ultimately mouldable for practical use.

It took another five years before he had worked out the processes required at an industrial level. He patented the invention in 1844. If he hadn't tried to deceive his wife...?

Another accidental domestic drama led to German chemist, Christian Schönbein, creating the modern explosives industry by discovering guncotton. Unknown to, and against the wishes of, his wife, Schönbein experimented in his kitchen in 1845 and accidentally spilt a mixture of nitric acid and sulphuric acid. He used his wife's cotton apron to mop up the mess, but when he hung it up it caught fire spontaneously as it dried out.

He had, unwittingly, converted the cellulose in the cotton apron into nitrocellulose. As it heated and dried, it oxidised spectacularly. It was to be several decades before a way was developed to manufacture the stuff safely, but by the 1890s guncotton had replaced gunpowder as the standard base for modern military ammunition.

Elisha Gray is a name unknown to us today. But it could have been as famous as Alexander Graham Bell, for Gray is, on the evidence, the true inventor of the telephone. He just messed up a bit on presentation and was disadvantaged by an incredible chance encounter by his opponent.

Gray's design for the telephone actually worked better than Bell's. They both applied for their patents on the same day, Valentine's Day 1876, Gray just a few hours after Bell and putting in a *caveat* – a detailed notice of intention to file – rather than the full technical description. Although not a complete application, it was nonetheless a powerful enough method to protect Gray's claim to be the inventor.

Officials decided they would scrutinise both applicants' work to determine who had proper claim on the invention. While Gray stayed at home in Chicago, Bell was more assertive, travelling from his Canadian home in Ontario, whence he had emigrated from Scotland, to Washington and pressed his case personally with the Patent Office.

By chance, the patent official Bell saw turned out to have a lot in common with him. He was reportedly a deaf mute. (Bell had started his work on telephony through the family's interest in working with the deaf and teaching speech to them.) According to one account, the official showed Bell Gray's design, which had a better method for transmitting sound. Bell wrote Gray's mechanism in the margin of his own patent. Bell's first practical working telephone had Gray's version of the sound transmitter.

The Patent Office decided in Bell's favour. Gray discovered the dubious additions by Bell, tried to challenge the patent award in court but eventually settled for a modest cash compensation and signed away all his claims to the telephone.

Two curious footnotes to the saga of who invented the telephone have emerged in recent years. In June 2002, the US Congress passed a resolution formally recognising Italian-American immigrant, Antonio Meucci, as the true inventor. Meucci is said to have developed a working model as early as 1870 – six years before Bell and Gray – and filed notice of the impending patent application in 1871. He was simply too poor to renew the claim when it expired in 1874, allowing Bell to trump him two years later.

Even more strangely, the London Science Museum reported in December 2003 that evidence had been found in its archives that a telephone device invented in 1863 by German inventor, Philipp Reis, actually worked. Tests were conducted on the device in March 1947 by engineers from the British firm Standard Telephone and Cables which demonstrated its efficacy, and proving Reis to be the true inventor of the telephone. However, the results were suppressed by the chairman of STC because the company was then bidding for a contract with, ironically, the American Telephone and Telegraph company (AT&T, which had evolved out of Bell's original company) and it was feared that the claims would jeopardise the company's chances. All the files relating to the tests were secreted away in STC and only returned to the Science Museum in 1955, where they then lay undiscovered for half a century.

The development of the direct-dial telephone system, eliminating the operator, arose from a distinctly unsocial motive: an undertaker suspected that a female operator at the local exchange was directing business callers to her husband's (or other stories have it, her lover's) firm, a rival undertaker.

Almon Strowger, a mortician and electrical tinkerer then living in Missouri, patented the automatic exchange in 1891 in response, and the world's first working direct-dial service began in his then home town of La Porte, Indiana, the following year. His frustrations at misdirected calls and lost business presumably ceased as records show he died a wealthy individual 10 years later.

The phonograph was a direct and unexpected offshoot of the telephone. One immediate development after the telephone's invention was customers' demand for a way of obtaining a permanent record of their conversation. In the summer of 1877, history's other great inventor, Thomas Edison, was tinkering with telephone speakers when he noticed that the diaphragm of the speaker reverberated in tandem with the sound. He fixed a stylus to the speaker and saw how when he shouted at the speaker the stylus created a unique groove on waxed paper placed underneath it. It could then replay back the same sound.

From there he developed the wax cylinder recording device which, by accident, would become the forerunner of the vinyl record. The original intention was entirely for servicing the commercial world, replacing paper as the medium for recording agreements and contracts. However, in practice, the wax was fragile, the recording poor quality and they could not survive too many transits in the mail.

So manufacturers of the devices looked for other uses. In 1889, the first coin-operated phonograph was installed in an arcade in San Francisco. For a nickel, listeners could hear a two-minute musical recording. To the makers' astonishment, that single machine took $1,000 in five months. Thus the recorded music industry was born.

By 1894, the more recognisably modern seven-inch gramophone record was on sale. Within five years, nearly three million records had been sold in the United States, and recorded music had become the most popular entertainment medium of all time.

The name James Swinburne might have been better known to the world had he not been overcautious about getting his invention patented. The 49-year-old Scottish-born chemist had developed the process for creating the world's first plastic in his London laboratory in 1907. When he finally went to secure his patent rights, he discovered he had been beaten to it by Belgian Leo Baekeland, who had invented his version, Bakelite. Baekeland had been awarded the patent for his identical product...only the day before.

The inventor of the thermos flask saw no commercial purpose to his idea and never patented it. His assistant took the concept and made millions.

James Dewar invented the double-walled vessel that kept its contents at a steady temperature because of the vacuum between the inner and outer walls, in 1892. As a practising chemist pioneering in the liquefaction of gases, he wanted it for purely scientific purposes, to provide a device for sustained cooling.

One of his students, Reinhold Burger, instead saw the commercial potential of keeping contents hot, and began making the device in Germany in 1904 for domestic use, under the patented trade name *thermos*, the Greek for heat. The Thermos company, which still holds the rights to the invention, has been making millions from the idea ever since.

James Dewar remained a Cambridge chemistry don until the

end of his life, co-invented the explosive cordite and ended up with a knighthood, but little monetary wealth.

Heroin was created in 1897 as a patent cough remedy. Its inventor, Heinrich Dreser of the German pharmaceutical company, Bayer, had also that year invented aspirin, which he thought was less effective than this second compound he had discovered. His notes record him as believing that aspirin would be counterproductive to a body trying to recover from an ailment as it had an 'enfeebling' effect on the heart. In contrast, in the tests he conducted on himself and fellow workers, he found that his second discovery, a derivative of morphine, had a 'heroic' effect.

With little further testing, the drug was commercially released in November 1898 under the brand name Heroin. Advertisements claimed it was 10 times more effective on colds than codeine with only a tenth of the toxic effects, and more effective than morphine as a painkiller. It was marketed as the era's wonder drug.

Within a year, heroin was being used in all types of elixir medicines – there were heroin pastilles, heroin cough lozenges, heroin water-soluble salts. It was particularly popular in the United States. An authoritative medical journal in Boston published an editorial in 1900, saying, 'It possesses many advantages over morphine. It's not hypnotic, and there's no danger of acquiring a habit.' In the next six years, at least 180 clinical studies were published on heroin around the world, nearly all of them favourable.

It was not long before reports began filtering back of consumers who had become 'immune' to the new drug, and needed increasingly strong doses. It still took until 1913 for Bayer to stop making it as a medicine. By then, a flood of hospital admissions in America had begun to reveal an alarming new phenomenon of mass addiction.

Ole Evinrude, a Norwegian immigrant to Wisconsin, is credited as the inventor of the first commercially successful outboard motor for boats – and all because his girlfriend asked for an ice cream.

He came up with the need in 1906 when, according to his account, he found himself rowing a five-mile round trip in 90-degree heat for the ice cream while on holiday on an island in Lake Michigan. By the time he had returned, the ice cream had completely melted.

By the next summer he had developed a one-and-a-half horse-power engine weighing 62 pounds. With further refinement, by 1911 he had registered his patent and formed a business partnership with a manufacturer. He continued to develop better and more powerful engines until his death in 1934.

According to research published in 1998, an obscure British mathematician probably developed the concept of general relativity at least 40 years before Albert Einstein. Papers belonging to William Kingdon Clifford, a professor at University College London, were discovered which showed that in the 1870s he had formulated the same concepts of the relationship between space, matter and gravity as Einstein put together only in 1915.

Clifford had been a mathematical prodigy, and become professor at just 26. Clifford's fate as a forgotten pioneer lay in the hostility his strange ideas provoked among his colleagues, who regarded him as a mad eccentric who was best ignored, and his early death from tuberculosis in 1879, aged only 33. He died just 11 days before Einstein was born.

Had Clifford lived longer, he might well have developed ideas beyond the theory we now know as relativity. As one promoter of Clifford's cause remarked in 1998, 'Just imagine what might have been achieved if the mature Clifford had met with the young Einstein.'

Alexander Fleming discovered the principles behind penicillin in 1922 by having a cold. The bacteriologist was preparing culture dishes for an entirely unrelated experiment when a drip from his nose fell into the dish. Annoyed that this had spoiled his culture, he put it to one side as a wasted effort. He noticed days later that the mucus had killed off bacteria in the dish wherever it had come into contact with it. Fleming isolated the active agent in the mucus – lysozyme – the antibacterial substance found in saliva and nasal mucus, but this was not strong enough against the bacteria that caused real illness in humans. He dropped the thought.

It might never have been resurrected had chance not intervened again in 1928. Fleming had grown cultures of staphylococci bacteria in dishes that he left on his desk when he went on holiday. One version of the story has it that his assistant left the window open overnight. He discovered on returning that mould had contaminated the dishes. Where the mould had grown it had destroyed the bacteria.

The mould was a rare one, *Penicillium*, being grown in the laboratory immediately below Fleming's. By an amazing accident, it seems that spores had travelled between the two labs. Fleming recognised the antibacterial effect as similar to his accidental discovery six years before. It prompted him to identify the mould, but not being a chemist he did little to pursue the potential further. He had no idea he had discovered one of the 20th century's most valuable medical advances.

It was 1940 before others, drawing on Fleming's account, developed penicillin into a usable medicine.

Frank Whittle, inventor of the jet engine, patented his first working design while a flying instructor with the RAF in 1930 at the age of only 22. Had the Air Ministry exploited the idea straight away, who knows how far the possession of jet-powered fighters might have affected Britain's military balance with Germany in the 1930s. At the time, however, no official interest was shown.

Incredibly, not only did the Ministry show no interest in Whittle's ideas, the authorities also failed to classify his patent. In 1932, it was published to the world.

Both Germany (in August 1939) and Italy (in August 1940) beat the RAF to developing the world's first jet aircraft. Not until June 1939 was the Gloster company asked to develop an experimental aircraft. Within two years, in May 1941, the Gloster E28/39 flew successfully.

Ironically, it was then wartime shortages that hindered further development of the craft until almost the end of the war when, in 1944, the twin-jet Meteor made its appearance. What might have been...?

Copying of a more sinister kind enabled Soviet Russia to obtain its first long-range nuclear bomber after the Second World War through the misplaced assumptions of an American air crew.

At the time, only the United States had the capacity to deliver a nuclear weapon. It had done so twice on Japan in 1945 to end the war using its strategic B-29 Superfortress bomber. As the wartime alliance broke down, an anxious Stalin was told he had been presented with a golden gift. Three B-29s had made forced landings in late 1944 at Vladivostock in the far east of Siberia, choosing Soviet territory over Chinese as they still believed Russia was an ally. It was to prove a calamitous mistake.

It emerged only in 2001 how Stalin's aircraft designer, Andrei Tupolev, took apart one of the B-29s 'rivet by rivet' and measured and photographed every single one of its 105,000 components. Making 40,000 drawings, Tupolev produced a Russian version, the Tu-4, which was displayed at Moscow's Aviation Day air show as quickly as August 1947.

With his atomic spies also active, within another two years Stalin also had his own nuclear bomb to go with it. His strategic position had been secured against the West.

But for a tragic accident, Britain could well hold the distinction of being home to the world's first manned, powered, heavier-than-air flight.

In 1896, Percy Sinclair Pilcher, who had long experimented with gliders in the small village of Eynsford in Kent, set out ideas in his extraordinary Patent 9144 that is considered by aviation historians to be the world's first practical design for a powered aircraft.

By the summer of 1899 he had designed an engine that was both light enough but also powerful enough to power the craft. It was at a time when the Wrights had only just decided to start experimenting with gliders. Pilcher's engine generated 4hp but weighed only 40lb. He then commissioned an engineer to build it.

Then, so tantalisingly close, fate intervened. Always anxious to demonstrate his machines, Pilcher accepted an invitation from a friend, Lord Braye, to display his glider, the *Hawk*, at the peer's Leicestershire home. In the grounds at Market Harborough on 30 September 1899, he was flying at 30ft when a small rod in the tail of his craft broke and he crashed, seriously injuring himself. He lingered for two days. When he died on 2 October, aged just 32, the dreams of a British first flight disappeared with him.

History's accolade for inventing powered, sustained and controlled heavier-than-air flight would go elsewhere. But for Pilcher's infectious wish to share his dreams with others, it would almost certainly have been very different and it would have been the *Eynsford Hawk*, not Kitty Hawk, the site of the Wrights' first powered flight in North Carolina, that would occupy premier place in the annals of aviation.

As if to wallow in Britain's closeness to fame, in 2003, to mark the centenary of the first manned flight, enthusiasts built a replica of the *Hawk*. It flew for 38 seconds – three times longer than the Wrights' first effort.

A computer reconstruction in 2003 of the Wrights' first flight to mark the 100th anniversary revealed that the flight came perilously close to failure. It had worked only because of a combination of fortunate weather and Wilbur Wright getting his sums wrong.

The reconstruction had been ordered to satisfy the American Institute of Aeronautics and Astronautics' health and safety requirements for flying an exact replica of the Wright plane on the centenary. Analysts discovered that the flight was saved from stalling only because of the higher efficiency of the propeller than Wilbur had calculated, coupled with winds blowing from the right direction and at precisely the right speed.

The Wright Flyer was 75lb heavier than originally designed, but was saved by the unexpected performance from the propeller. As a result, the replica was required to fly significantly faster than the 30mph achieved in the real flight – to prevent it from catastrophically stalling.

In the event, bad weather and high winds prevented the replica achieving any lift-off at all at the ceremonial commemoration on 17 December 2003.

Ralph Alpher, the American physicist behind the Big Bang theory of the creation of the universe, became a forgotten man in the annals of scientific discovery all because his boss thought up a clever joke.

In April 1948, he had become the first to set out the mathematical model that showed how the Big Bang led to the reactions that formed all the chemical elements. He enjoyed fleeting fame, and his supervisor at George Washington University, George Gamow, set him to produce a second paper – on how radiation from the Big Bang should still be detectable – a few months later. Although Alpher did all the work, Gamow, a noted physicist himself, thought it would be amusing to add his name and that of another famous scientist in the field, Hans Bethe, producing an authors' line-up of Alpher, Bethe, Gamow – a pun on the Greek letters alpha, beta, gamma – highly appropriate, he thought, for a work which described the beginnings of the universe.

Unfortunately for Alpher, because both the others were world-renowned names, the scientific community assumed that it was they who had done most of the research. Alpher's starring role in the discovery was rapidly forgotten as a result. When, in 1964, two astronomers detected the radiation Alpher had predicted, confirming the Big Bang theory, they won the Nobel Prize. Alpher's contribution was completely ignored. He bitterly tried to stake his claim for recognition, but to no avail.

By then, the disappointed Alpher had long left the academic science field and spent most of the rest of his career in the research and development department of the General Electric company. He died in obscurity in 2007.

❦

James Chadwick, one of the world's foremost pioneers of nuclear science, became a physicist by mistake. He intended to be a mathematician but as a 16-year-old joined the wrong queue at Manchester University in 1907 and found himself enrolled in physics instead.

He stayed because he was impressed by the tutor who interviewed him: Ernest Rutherford, who would go on to work out the structure of the atom. Chadwick would work under Rutherford for much of his career, uncovering the fundamentals of atomic structures, and discovering the neutron particle in 1932. During the Second World War he led the British team of scientists working on the American project to build the atomic bomb.

And all because he once stood in the wrong line.

It was to be one of Rutherford's mistakes – and an enforced wait at traffic lights – that would lead to the discovery of the darkest secret of the atom. The concept of a nuclear chain reaction, which led to the development of the atomic bomb, came to Hungarian scientist Leó Szilárd as he stood waiting for the lights to change on a London street on the morning of 12 September 1933.

Szilárd had just read a report in that day's *Times* of a lecture by Rutherford to the annual meeting of the British Association. The pioneer of understanding the mysteries of the atom had dismissed Szilárd's idea of the possibilities of releasing the energy from atoms. Rutherford had called it 'moonshine'. Irritated by this, and the rain that had just started to fall while he waited to cross Southampton Row, the spark of inspiration hit him. He conceived how one atom bombarding another could release two particles which would go on to release four ... As he crossed the road, he later recalled, the notion of nuclear fission was laid out before him in his mind.

Szilárd patented the idea the following year, but chose the wrong element to experiment with. He failed to produce a successful chain reaction in practice. He teamed up with Enrico Fermi and the pair discovered in 1939 that uranium was the perfect material for producing easily released particles. They went on to create the first controlled nuclear chain reaction in December 1942 as part of the American Manhattan Project to build the atomic bomb.

Robert FitzRoy, captain of the *Beagle* survey ship which would take Charles Darwin on his, and science's, epoch-making voyage, nearly refused to accept Darwin because of the shape of his nose.

FitzRoy was an amateur adherent of phrenology, the belief that a person's character is revealed in the shape of their head. He was suspicious at first of Darwin's rather broad, squat, nose, which he thought reflected a lazy disposition and a weak character – hardly the right fit for such a prolonged and lonely journey where the pair would be the only two gentlemen aboard. But as he dined with Darwin at that first meeting, he relented and offered him the berth.

Darwin had still not been FitzRoy's first choice. He only got his chance because the captain's preferred selection dropped out. He had also had to overcome resolute opposition to the voyage from his own father, who wanted him to go into the church. 'You will be a disgrace to yourself and all your family' and the voyage would be 'a useless undertaking' were his verdicts. But he was persuaded by the rest of the family to concede.

As he sailed, Darwin could justifiably feel that he had already overcome three small but potentially fatal obstacles to his hoped-for future.

Hubert Cecil Booth, the Gloucester-born inventor of the vacuum cleaner, nearly killed himself with his first experiment to test his concept before he had ever put together a working model.

He was inspired in 1901 to 'suck, not blow' by seeing a demonstration of an American machine for cleaning train carriages which used a high pressure air jet to blow dust out of fabrics. In a restaurant afterwards, it struck him that a more effective method would be to try to suck the dust up. He put his handkerchief on an old chair and breathed in heavily. He nearly choked to death on the dust.

Within months, the vacuum cleaner was born.

Science fiction writer Arthur C. Clarke, who is credited with coming up with the idea of global communications through orbiting satellites, made no financial gain from his breakthrough thought since he wrote about his notion in a magazine article in *Wireless World* in October 1945 rather than taking out a patent for his innovation. He may have deprived himself of millions of pounds from royalties.

The Hubble space telescope, launched in 1990 at a cost of over $2 billion was quickly discovered to have a major problem – its pictures were blurred. The distortion was found to have been caused by a speck of paint on an optical measuring rod during the polishing of the primary mirror. This had led to the lens being 0.002 millimetres too flat – one fiftieth the width of a human hair.

It made all the difference though. It would take three years, an $86 million repair bill and a Shuttle mission in 1993 to put it right.

Hubble was not space's first catastrophic glitch caused by a minuscule oversight. NASA's Mariner I mission to Venus in June 1962 had to be aborted when the rocket went off course four minutes after take-off. The investigation discovered that the cause of the failure was the omission of a single hyphen in the flight computer's software program. The punctuation error had cost NASA $18.5 million (about $400 million in today's values).

Nearly 40 years later, it seemed that elementary slip-ups could still happen. NASA's Mars Climate Orbiter was lost in September 1999 as it headed into a far lower orbit than planned which led it to burning up in the atmosphere. An investigation discovered that computer software written by separate parts of the mission team were in different units of measurement for key navigation operations. The propulsion team had used English imperial units (feet, inches) to specify thrust while the navigation team had used the data as if it was in the metric system.

It led the probe to be 100 kilometres lower in orbit than

intended. The mission had cost $125 million. Said NASA's associate administrator, Edward Weiler, 'People sometimes make errors.'

NASA's $260 million three-year Genesis project to collect space dust from the Sun on wafer-thin glass platelets appeared to end catastrophically when the capsule's parachute failed to work on re-entry in September 2004. Instead of a smooth landing, it crashed into the Utah desert at 100mph. It was later discovered that the parachute had not deployed because the deceleration sensors, which should have triggered it, had been designed upside down.

On opening the samples, however, scientists later reassured the world that they appeared to have survived the impact.

The apparently smooth and trouble-free first manned landing on the Moon in July 1969 was in fact plagued with last-second computer glitches that nearly turned the mission into a disaster. Two unexplained computer warnings in three minutes as the Apollo 11 lander dropped to 2,500ft above the Moon's surface caused Neil Armstrong to take manual control of the landing much earlier than scheduled.

Although Mission Control told the astronauts to ignore the warnings – they were later found to be indicating a general overloading of systems – they did affect the drift of the descent and the lunar lander was nearly four miles further on than it should have been, and only two miles within the limit set for a mandatory abort.

As Armstrong struggled at 200ft to find a safe new landing spot, he had barely 60 seconds of descent fuel left. Had he run out, the landing would have been too heavy for the fragile craft and if they were not killed in the impact they would not have been able to take off again from a damaged platform.

Exactly how much fuel remained when he did land was never determined. According to co-pilot Buzz Aldrin, his instruments showed just 10 seconds' worth of fuel were left. After their four-and-a quarter day odyssey to get there, they had had at the end barely a few heartbeats to get it right first time.

The reason for the computer overload was discovered during the astronauts' stay on the surface. A radar on the lander, used for tracking the orbiting command module, had been left on automatic, meaning that the computer was using valuable memory analysing data from itself. Mission Control realised the mistake just 30 minutes before the lander was due to blast back off into orbit and instructed the crew to turn it to manual. Had it been left on as before, they would have encountered the same computer failings during the even more hazardous re-docking manoeuvre that could have ended in a catastrophic contrast so soon after the success of the landing itself.

NASA intended an elegantly symbolic ending to the mission, but was thwarted by earthly political rivalries. They planned to signify the completion of the historic pledge by President Kennedy in 1961 to achieve a Moon landing before the decade was out by having the Apollo 11 crew picked up by the aircraft carrier *John F. Kennedy*. But Richard Nixon's deep-seated jealousy of his now dead rival intervened and he vetoed the plan. He insisted on sending a different carrier, the *USS Hornet.*

Few of the other Moon missions escaped hitches that almost brought the flights to terminal disaster. *Apollo 12* was struck by lightning twice within 16 seconds on launch. The first discharged right through the spacecraft and on to the launch tower 6,000ft below. The second caused the command module's entire navigation system to go down, and disconnected the ship's batteries from the power system. According to one account, Pete Conrad, the flight commander, relayed to Mission Control 'in one breath, the longest list of malfunctions ever heard'. When they reached orbit, it took two and a half hours of checks before the flight was given the OK to continue.

When on the Moon, Conrad's partner Al Bean ruined all television coverage of man's second expedition when he pointed the camera into the sun and destroyed it. The only coverage of the mission was by radio and that did much to turn off the American public. The only photographic record comes from the stills taken by the astronauts themselves. (And they managed to leave a roll of pictures behind on the surface by mistake, having forgotten to pack it back on board.)

Conrad could have taken one of the most intriguing shots ever had his practical joke come off. He had smuggled an automatic timer for his stills camera on to the mission without the knowledge of Mission Control. He and Bean planned to take a picture of them both posing tourist-style in front of the lander. Conrad said he could not wait for the inevitable question asked by those back on Earth, 'Who took the snap?' He had hidden the timer in the rock box used to collect samples, and when it came to the moment to mount the shot, he could not find it amidst the stones. Realising he could only find it by emptying out the whole box, the pair decided to abandon the prank.

The explosion in the oxygen tank which crippled *Apollo 13* was caused by an oversight in the design of a thermostat on a heater which was equipped to run on only 28 volts, like the rest of the Apollo craft when it had first been designed. When the program upgraded the entire system to run at 65 volts, all components were upgraded to take the higher voltage – except someone forgot the heater. The thermostat was meant to keep the temperature of the oxygen tank at 80 degrees Fahrenheit. When it came into operation, the extra voltage melted its contacts shut and allowed the temperature in the tanks to rise to 1,000 degrees, cracking most of the insulation. No one on the ground knew because the controller's gauge at Mission Control only went up to 85 degrees. As the astronauts activated the fan for the tanks to do a regular control procedure, an electrical spark ignited the exposed plastic covering the wiring and, fuelled by the oxygen, caused the explosion.

The *Apollo 14* command module had so much difficulty docking with the lunar module as it tried to pluck it from its launch berth inside the Saturn V rocket, that the mission was nearly abandoned. After five attempts, and an hour and half of consultation with Mission Control, the two craft still failed to lock. The crew even planned to depressurise their module, open the docking hatch and drag the two craft together by hand. Eventually, they forced a firm contact by firing their thrusters as they docked to increase the pressure. It appeared to shake lose whatever had blocked the locking devices. It was barely an hour before the massive stage of the rocket would have vented its spare fuel – a procedure that required the command module to be a considerable distance away. It did, however, leave an anxious pall over the whole mission. No one knew what the fault had been, and they would have to repeat the docking after the Moon landing for a safe return.

On the same mission, as the lander was just 90 minutes from the Moon's surface, a faulty signal from the Mission Abort button came on. The astronauts were used to malfunctioning alarms, but this was potentially fatal. As soon as the descent engines had been fired, as they were about to do, activation of the alarm again would automatically abort the landing. It required programmers on the ground to rewrite the computer's software to instruct the system to ignore any signal from the errant alarm. The necessary changes were developed, signalled to the module and keyed in just 10 minutes before the descent engines had to be ignited or the mission aborted. Even as they neared the surface, a further potentially fatal problem occurred. By 32,000ft, the lunar lander's ground radar had still not started working. Without it, it was impossible to judge a landing. Mission rules specified that if it was not working by 10,000ft, it was a mandatory abort. On the advice of Mission Control, they effectively unplugged the system and plugged it back in again. They were under 20,000ft – and seconds from an abort – when the radar began operating.

Apollo 16 had separated and the lunar lander was en route to the surface when the orbiting command module's engine failed, threatening the mission. In order to ensure that the crew had a means of getting home, if the command module engine failed they would have to use the lunar module engine to fire them back to Earth. Flight rules dictated that the lander had to cease its descent and return to orbit with the command module until the problem was resolved. If it was not within 10 hours, the entire landing was off as they would be out of range of the planned landing site. The fault was rectified after six, giving them just sufficient time to complete a successful descent.

The main experiment on *Apollo 16* was one to measure heat flow under the Moon's surface, vital to geologists for understanding how the Moon had been formed. The first attempt to run the experiment had been lost when *Apollo 13* failed to reach the Moon, so NASA were doubly expectant this time. It carried a price tag of $1m. As Mission Commander John Young set up the base station, he failed to notice that the cable linking buried sensors to the device had looped around his boot. It was clearly visible to the ground audience watching on television, but before Mission Control could alert him he had hopped away, ripping out the line from the experiment and ruining this one too.

A curious omission from Alfred Nobel's choice of prizes may have been down to a simple affair of the heart.

When, in 1895, he wrote his instructions for creating annual prizes for achievement, Nobel specified precisely the five areas – physics, chemistry, medicine, literature and peace. Some have pondered ever since the strange absence of a prize for mathematics, the essential building block of the sciences.

One theory has it that a mathematician stole the heart of one of Nobel's mistresses. A letter exists which implies that a notable Swedish mathematics professor, Gosta Mittag-Leffler, believed that the absence of a prize in his discipline was down to the personal estrangement between the two men.

A related theory points to the attempts by the professor, as Nobel was formulating his own plans for prizes, to persuade him to donate his wealth to the professor's own institution which offered a mathematics award. Could overzealous lobbying have turned Nobel off too, especially if he harboured suspicions about Mittag-Leffler for other reasons?

Nobel's lifelong antipathy towards lawyers nearly destroyed his entire scheme even before it got off the ground. He drew up his will entirely without legal advice, leaving many elements of his grand plan unclear and open to challenge in the courts. He had never established a legal place of residence, and with so much of his wealth spread around the world the executor of his will had to work overtime to establish legal ownership of the amassed fortune and return it to Sweden. Nor, before he died, had Nobel actually established the foundation to which the funds were to be left.

Members of Nobel's family, who were embittered at the prospect of losing an inheritance, tried to have the plans overturned on the grounds that as the funds did not legally have an owner, they were the rightful heirs. They failed.

The idea also attracted opposition from the King of Sweden who objected, along with much of public opinion. He scathingly questioned the idea of Swedish wealth being dispersed to foreigners at a time when Sweden was a poor country. He eventually changed his mind years later when he decided that the annual prize giving might bring beneficial publicity for Sweden.

The machine that most reshaped domestic lives in the late 20th century, the microwave oven, emerged accidentally from a chocolate bar and wartime work in radar which used magnetrons to generate the microwaves used to detect objects.

A radar researcher at the Raytheon Corporation, Percy Spencer, who wandered across a magnetron beam in his lab in 1946 found the bar in his pocket had melted. Intrigued, he experimented by putting popcorn kernels near the magnetron tube and watched them pop. Next day he tried an egg, which exploded over a colleague.

By the end of 1946, Raytheon had patented the concept of a microwave oven, and in 1947 produced the first commercial device. There was some way to go before it was ready for every home to have one: the first version was nearly 6ft tall, weighed a third of a ton and cost $5,000.

The jacuzzi was born because a member of the seven-brother Jacuzzi family had developed rheumatoid arthritis. The clan, California immigrants from Italy, had established a profitable business making air pumps for aircraft. In 1948, Candido Jacuzzi's six-year-old son needed therapy for his increasingly debilitating condition. He developed a portable pump to immerse in a hospital bath to soothe the child's limbs. By 1955, the idea was launched commercially as a therapeutic device and within 15 years the first made-for-purpose whirlpool baths with fixed air jets came on to the market.

The boy, Kenneth Jacuzzi, went on to successfully run the company that had been born to ease his childhood affliction.

Sylvan Goldman, a store owner in Oklahoma City, came up with the idea of the shopping trolley in 1936 from the chance observation that his customers tended to stop shopping not because they had everything they had come for but because their hand-held baskets became too heavy.

The idea of a wheeled cart came to him in his office as he stared at a foldaway metal chair. He patented a double-decker, pram-like contraption the following year. He then encountered customer resistance. Men thought the device effeminate; women that they were unstylish (and too much like prams).

Goldman's stroke of genius was to hire models of all ages to pretend to be customers and walk around the store using the trolleys. The deception worked and by peer persuasion, the trolley caught on and Goldman made a $400 million fortune.

Swiss inventor of Velcro, George de Mestral, was inspired from a walk in the Jura mountains in 1941 when his dog brushed against cockleburrs. As he tried to remove them he was intrigued by their tenacious grip. He took one of the burrs back to his amateur laboratory and under the microscope saw the tiny hooks that enable the burr to cling to any soft material.

He patented Velcro in 1955, taking the name from a combination of *velour* for loop and *crochet* for the hook.

The now ubiquitous 'post-it' note was a chance invention born of the combination of the needs of a church chorister and his work colleague's experiment that had resulted in a product with no apparent practical use.

Art Fry, a chemist at the 3M company, in Minnesota in 1974 encountered a problem with finding the right place in his hymn book as he sang in two services on a Sunday. He would use a paper slip to mark the places of the hymns for both services. By the second service, the slips had often fallen out after turning the pages for the first.

Fry recalled a strange concoction a colleague at 3M had produced six years earlier and shelved because no one could think of a practical use. Spencer Silver had developed a glue that did not quite stick. Fry spent a year and a half working out how it could be applied to the paper slips to produce a bookmark that stayed affixed when it was needed but could be pulled off without damaging the page when its work was done.

By 1977, Fry had mastered the technical problems and developed the concept of the removable note. Although the notes bombed when they first went on sale that year and were about to be judged a commercial failure – people would not lay out cash for a product there was no obvious use for – when free samples were sent out to offices for an extended trial, office workers began to find a multitude of uses for them that they had never previously thought of. Once practical uses had been discovered, 'post-it' notes, relaunched commercially in 1980, suddenly became an indispensable part of the office furniture.

'Blu-Tack', the sticky reusable adhesive, was an entirely accidental creation in 1971 as a by-product of a process being used by Bostik to try to develop a sealant. The lumpy, tacky material was too thick and not adhesive enough to be a sealant, but as company officials toyed with it, they found it useful to fix announcements to walls in the office. It was then noticed that when the announcements came down, the tacky stuff was still sticky and could be used again. 'Blu-Tack' was born as a commercial product and soon became another modern office essential.

The original substance was white. It was coloured blue because of fears that children might mistake it for a chewy sweet. There were no blue sweets on the market at the time.

The rawlplug – the sheath that helps to hold screws firmly in a wall – is only around today because of the British Museum's worries about its fragile decor. In 1919, engineer John Rawlings had been contracted to fix some electrical fittings to the walls of the museum, as unobtrusively as possible and without damaging the historic wall surfaces.

The traditional method of doing this was to gouge out a hole in the masonry and pack it with wood, which held the screw tightly in the wall. Rawlings was told he could not do this so he developed the plug (the first ones were thin brass, then a hemp and string blend). He named the device the Rawlplug, his company started manufacturing them in 1920 and it revolutionised the job of fixing things to walls.

The 'Band-Aid' plaster only came about because of the poor kitchen coordination techniques of a cotton buyer's wife. The buyer, Earle Dickson, worked for the Johnson & Johnson company, manufacturers of surgical gauze and adhesive tape. His newly married life was affected in 1920 by his wife's frequent accidents in preparing dinner. At the time, the accepted way of dressing a wound was to apply the gauze on the wound and use separate pieces of sticky tape to hold it in place. As Mrs Dickson needed so many, Earle prepared treatments in advance. He laid out a long strip of tape and at regular intervals laid a piece of gauze on it. Whenever Mrs Dickson needed a dressing, she simply cut off a strip of tape containing a piece of gauze.

Earle Dickson suddenly realised how easier dressing small wounds could be, and the plaster was born. The following year, Johnson & Johnson produced their first commercial version. Rivals Smith & Nephew produced their 'Elastoplast' three years later.

Earle eventually became a Vice President of Johnson & Johnson. As the company's history relates, no one actually knows, however, whether Mrs Dickson, who started it all, ever mastered the art of accident-free cooking.

The flexible contact lens was invented through a chance conversation on a Czech train in 1952 between a chemist and a passenger who was reading a scientific paper on corrective eye surgery. The chemist was Otto Wichterle, an assistant professor at Prague University specialising in manmade fibres. The man he struck up a conversation with was a complete stranger to him, but as they talked about the problems of correcting vision, Wichterle offered his own thoughts about developing a plastic implant. The listener turned out to be an official with the Czech Health Ministry, and shortly afterwards Wichterle was commissioned to make good his idea.

It took another nine years before he had perfected a comfortable version. He initially ground his prototype lenses using a grinder adapted from the motor of a record player. He never acquired any wealth from the invention. The communist Czech government sold the rights to an American businessman for just $330,000.

One of the icons of modern security controls, the door lock system using a keypad and an entry code, was inspired by its inventor, Frenchman Bob Carrière, watching a Popeye cartoon with his children in the late 1960s.

The story showed a chef locking his fridge by using a telephone dial device and a code number. Carrière thought this could be a useful way of securing a house door, saving problems with carrying keys around. Instead of a dial, which looked likely to take too long to unlock, Carrière took inspiration from his typewriter and developed a 12-button box, which he patented in 1970, called the Digicode.

They became popular in multi-occupancy Parisian apartment blocks. Carrière's big break came when the computer giant IBM ordered 150 sets to protect its sites. The same touchpad technology used in the door locks spread into a wide range of other modern automated devices, such as vending machines and the ubiquitous cashpoint. And all stemmed from a chance viewing of a children's cartoon. Carrière died in 2007 having sold his Digicode company in 1995.

The cat's eye reflective road stud was literally inspired by a driver nearly running over a cat on a dark country road in 1933. Yorkshireman Percy Shaw was driving through dense fog near his home in Boothtown, near Halifax, when he had to swerve to avoid a cat in the middle of the road. Only the reflection from its eyes alerted him. It also stopped him from driving over a cliff – the near-accident happened on a dangerous bend.

Shaw was so struck by his close escape that the idea of permanent light-reflecting warnings for roads became his mission in life. Within a year, he had perfected the design and started his company, Reflecting Roadstuds Ltd in 1935.

The Ministry of Transport held a competition for rival designs, and after two years Shaw's were the only ones still in one piece. All his rivals had dropped out because their designs either could not stand the repeated shocks of being run over or they silted up, blocking the glass.

Shaw's ingenious twist was another inspiration drawn directly from cats' real eyes. He embedded his studs in a moveable holder so that when run over the glass depressed. When it rose again, it pushed against the rubber coating and wiped itself clean, just like a cat's eyelid.

The bane of the modern motorist, the single- and double-yellow line system for restricting parking, was developed by the Ministry of Transport in the mid-1950s only through a loophole in the law which allowed the marking of roads but prohibited that of pavements. Wilfred Hadfield, an MoT engineer charged with looking at ways to reduce congestion, came up with the idea of the gutter-side markings to draw attention to restrictions which up until then could only be placed rather inconspicuously as small signs on lampposts.

They were first tested in Putney High Street and brought into permanent use in Slough in 1956. The ministry announced the introduction of a comprehensive national scheme the following year.

Bob Switzer, the Ohio-born inventor of high-visibility fluorescent clothing, did so as the result of an accident when he was a teenager. Sometime in the early 1930s, he tripped and fell off a loading bay while lifting crates for the Safeway supermarket. This put him into a coma for several months and permanently damaged his sight. To aid his recuperation, he was confined for several more months in a darkened room. The only stimulant for him was his collection of fluorescent minerals. After his recovery, he continued experimenting with fluorescent colours and working out how to create paints and dyes which glowed in the dark and reflected brightly in normal light.

By 1946, he had founded the company in Cleveland that later became the DayGlo Color Corporation. All high-visibility products around today, from security guard jackets and cyclists' safety strips to traffic cones, derive from the innovations developed by Bob Switzer.

He had dreamed of being a doctor, but his accident put paid to that. His invention though has perhaps gone on to save more lives than he could ever have managed as a solitary physician.

The inventor of the cashpoint machine never made a penny profit from his idea. He refused to patent the invention because he feared thieves would learn from it how to cheat the machine.

John Shepherd-Barron, head of security company De La Rue's armoured cash delivery operations which supplied cash to banks, was inspired by his own frustration of not being able to get his money out of the bank other than during working hours and a chocolate bar dispenser. The cash machine he devised was not the card-operated system familiar today. Bizarrely, in view of the problem it was trying to solve of not having to go into the bank while it was open, it relied on pre-purchasing a voucher from the bank that was then inserted into the machine to release the cash.

The system was bought by Barclays, and the first cash dispenser opened at its branch in Enfield, North London, in 1967. The other invention it required – the Personal Identification Number or PIN – was also created by Shepherd-Barron. He asked his wife, Caroline, what was the most number of digits she could readily remember as a security code. It turned out to be four.

6

Chance Beginnings

We would be driving Horchs today had it not been for the inability of the German car manufacturer, August Horch, to patch up a quarrel with his company backers. He was an irascible character, and preferred to leave his company to start another rather than make up, but could not use his own name any more because the original company retained the rights to it.

So Horch used the Latin translation of his name (which in German means 'hear') and produced in 1909 the first Audi.

The most famous aircraft of World War Two, the Spitfire, also got its name because of an argument. The plane's designer by chance overheard the head of the company building the aircraft having a furious row with his daughter.

Sir Robert McLean, chairman of Vickers, was heard to remark, 'There goes my little spitfire,' after his daughter, Annie, had stormed out of the room. Reginald Mitchell, the plane's designer, was present, liked the sound of it and the name stuck.

The design team were struggling to come up with a name for the craft. Had they not, it might have been the Shrike or the Shrew, names suggested by the Air Ministry.

According to some accounts, perhaps apocryphal, the Cunard liner *Queen Mary* would have been called the *Queen Victoria* but for a misplaced remark from which there was no way out.

Shortly before its launch in 1934, Sir Thomas Royden, one of the company directors, told King George V of the plan to name the ship 'after the greatest queen this country has ever known.' The King is said to have replied, 'Oh, my wife *will* be pleased.' So *Queen Mary* it had to be.

The bikini was so-named by its French designer, Louis Reard, since it was unveiled to the world in July 1946 four days after the first post-war American nuclear test had taken place on Bikini atoll in the Pacific. A rival designer, Jacques Heim, had beaten him to the mark bringing out a two-piece swimsuit, calling it in a blaze of publicity the *atome*. This had nothing to do with the tests, but from the atom being the smallest known article of matter.

Needing something different, three weeks later when he launched his, Reard plumped for *bikini*, as the 'ultimate' creation because of the current headlines, and it was that name that curiously stuck. Had they been launched another year, or even another month, bathers might be sunbathing in *atomes* instead.

The scriptwriter for the television series *Dr Who*, Terry Nation, forcefully turned down the BBC's original request to him to write for the children's series. He thought the idea beneath him. Later, without a job, he found that his agent had decided not to pass on his ill-tempered refusal to the corporation. He was hired without demur.

Asked to develop an arch-enemy for the Doctor, he was responsible for one of television's most famous creations, the Daleks. He got the name from glancing at his bookshelf while trying to conjure a sufficiently threatening moniker. He is said to have noticed his set of encyclopaedias, and took inspiration from one of the volumes that covered topics from DAL-EK. The BBC, however, officially discounts the tale. It maintains that he simply made up the explanation to put an end to the persisistent questioning about the origin of the name.

A similar tale is told of Frank Baum, author of *The Wizard of Oz*. He published the story in 1900. The origin of Oz is said to have come from Baum looking up while trying to think of a name for his fictional world and his eyes alighting on a filing cabinet draw labelled O-Z.

Another theory has it that it was drawn from his home state of New York, OZ each being the letters following on from NY. (In the same way as Arthur C. Clarke is said to have derived HAL, the name of the computer in *2001: A Space Odyssey* from shifting each letter one backwards from the computer manufacturer, IBM.)

One of Hollywood's iconic attractions – the forecourt of Grauman's Chinese Theatre on Hollywood Boulevard – where movie stars have been immortalising their handprints and footprints in the pavement, began entirely by accident when owner Sid Grauman stepped into some wet cement outside the entrance in 1927, a year after he had opened the place. He realised how unique the mark was and how permanent it could be.

Silent era star Mary Pickford was a partner in the theatre and, according to Grauman's own account, he asked her to put her footprint down, along with his other business partner, Douglas Fairbanks Jnr. The project steamrollered from there.

(Another account maintains that silent star Norma Talmadge was responsible for giving Grauman the idea by stepping into the setting concrete herself. However, she is officially recorded as registering her mark three weeks after the supposed first imprints by Pickford and Fairbanks Jnr. The truth is far from clear, and it's entirely possible that Grauman's partners insisted on trumping the starlet to be the first to be immortalised on the street.)

There are now nearly 250 imprints of almost every Hollywood hero's hands or feet, as well as two horse stars – Trigger and Champion ('the Wonder Horse') and the imprints of the *Stars Wars* robots, as well as scrawled autographs. It was a supreme business move too. The theatre became the most popular place to hold movie premieres.

The Sheraton hotel chain was so-named because of a single expensive sign. In 1939, the two-man partnership of Ernest Henderson and Robert Moore bought their third hotel. All had different names – the Stonehaven in Springfield, Massachusetts, Lee House in Washington and their newest acquisition in Boston, the Sheraton.

The Sheraton had a huge neon sign advertising itself. The partners thought this would be far too expensive to replace, so the entire chain became Sheratons to save on the expense.

One of the most famous children's books, Dr Seuss' *Green Eggs and Ham*, was written as a result of a bet that the author could not write an entire book using only 50 different words.

The inspiration for the most famous brand of map books in Britain – the *London A-Z* – came to 29-year-old Phyllis Pearsall in 1935 when she found herself misdirected by the only London street map then readily available, and discovered it had been last updated in 1918.

She walked 3,000 miles over the next year, rising at 5am and working for 18 hours a day, to list all 23,000 London streets.

When published in 1936, only a sharp-eyed printer saved the first edition from a calamitous error. Owing to an 'accident with a shoebox', the index almost left out Trafalgar Square. The compositor asked whether it was deliberate that there were no 'Tr-' entries.

Our historic imperial measurement of the foot (12 inches) was decreed by the length of Henry I's arm. The 11th century English monarch declared the foot would be one-third of his arm's length, which was 36 inches.

Tweed got its name by a miscommunication between a Scottish weaver and a London tailor. The weaver, identified in accounts only as coming from Hawick in the Scottish border country, sent a sample of his new twilled – diagonally ribbed – cloth to the London tailor, James Locke, in 1832. He described his product in the Scotch vernacular, 'tweeled', which Locke misread as 'tweed'. The name stuck.

The designer of the iconic red British telephone kiosk, Sir Giles Gilbert Scott, took its squared-bodied and domed roof shape from the tomb of Sir John Soane, one of the country's greatest architects. When trying to come up with a design for the competition run by the Post Office in 1924, he had just become a trustee of the Soane museum, which inspired the connection.

Britain's 999 emergency telephone number was introduced because of a single letter to *The Times* newspaper. In November 1935, one Norman Macdonald, a resident of Wimpole Street in London, wrote complaining at the difficulty he had encountered the day before in raising the alarm for a serious fire in the house opposite his in which five people died. He had attempted to call the fire brigade through the operator, but had had no response.

The government set up a committee to ponder the idea of a

dedicated telephone number for emergencies. Two years later, in June 1937, 999 was introduced in London, the first city in the world to have one.

Why 999, the longest number to complete in the days of dialling? 111 was rejected as it was thought it could easily be 'dialled' by mistake by wind blowing on telephone wires; 222 was already in use for a major exchange in the capital. 999 was picked simply because it did not then have a current use, and was memorable in an emergency.

The first advertising on British television did not come, as is officially recognised, on ITV's opening night in September 1955 (Gibbs SR toothpaste) but three years earlier through an accident on the BBC.

In the early 1950s, with television almost always broadcast live, an important accessory when broadcasting theatre was to have a suitably picturesque montage to put to camera when the performance broke for the interval. According to Paddy Russell, a stage manager for the play *Arrow to the Heart*, being broadcast on 20 July 1952, on this occasion a satchel of props had been arranged which included, he noticed, a jar of honey. All day he had been meaning to take the maker's label off the jar, but it was a busy production and he failed to do so.

At the interval, no one noticed the broadcast of the montage until halfway through when Russell passed a monitor. Recounting the incident in *Coming To You Live*, an oral history of early British television, he recalled, 'There was this jar of Gale's honey, straight-on to camera, right in the foreground. And that's how it stayed for five minutes! Five minutes! The first TV commercial in this country, and I suspect it's still the longest.'

One of British advertising's most enduring icons, the Andrex puppy, which has been selling toilet tissue to the nation since 1972, was a replacement concept for the company's original plan to have a child pull the toilet roll around the house. The authorities objected that it might encourage naughtiness in children, so the cute puppy was born instead.

Coca-Cola's most famous advertisement, launched in 1971 and featuring a multinational crowd on a hilltop singing 'I'd Like to Teach the World to Sing', was inspired by an enforced overnight stay at an Irish airport.

Bill Backer, the creative director for the advertising company that had the Coca-Cola account, was flying to London to work on songs for the new campaign when his plane was diverted to Shannon airport due to fog at Heathrow. He was forced to spend the night in the departure lounge where some of the passengers became angry at the disruption. By the morning, Backer later recalled, he saw many of the same people now smiling and laughing, and sharing stories over bottles of Coke.

He later described how in that moment 'I began to see a bottle of Coca-Cola as more than a drink. . . .[I] began to see the familiar words, "Let's have a Coke," as. . .actually a subtle way of saying, "Let's keep each other company for a little while." So that was the basic idea: to see Coke…as a tiny bit of commonality between all peoples, a universally liked formula that would help to keep them company for a few minutes.'

In writing the song, he told his lyricists, he did not know how it should start but he knew how it should end. That night he had scribbled down on an airline napkin the line that encapsulated his experience, 'I'd like to buy the world a Coke and keep it company.'

The ad ran unchanged for a phenomenal six years.

The popular belief that spinach has ingredients that particularly help to make people strong, propagated by the Popeye cartoons in the 1930s, developed because a German scientist investigating the iron content of vegetables in 1870 put a decimal point in the wrong place in his paper. His results suggested that spinach contained 10 times the amount of iron than it actually does. The mistake was not uncovered until 1937, by which time Popeye's popularity had made it impossible to overturn the myth.

The croissant, the archetypal symbol of French culinary fare, is, in fact, of Austrian origin, and began its life as a propaganda tool to mark the deliverance of the Austrian empire from the hands of the Muslim Turks.

It takes its crescent shape from the moon depicted on the Turkish flag, and is said to date from the siege of Vienna in 1683 when it was the local bakers who, while working through the night, heard the sounds of Turks tunnelling into the city and raised the alarm, thus saving the city and the empire. It was the furthest advance Muslim forces have ever made into Europe. The bakers created the special bun in the now familiar crescent design to celebrate victory over their religious rivals.

The first documented reference, incidentally, in French to the croissant dates only from 1853.

The strength of the modern Canadian economy can be traced back to the consequences of a rogue fox pestering a country blacksmith in 1903.

In the small hamlet of Cobalt in northern Ontario, Fred La Rose was being irritated by a red fox, which was sniffing round his workshop. According to tradition, he threw a hammer at the fox, which missed but struck a nearby outcrop of rock. It gleamed brightly and La Rose had discovered Canada's (and the world's) richest seam of silver.

The Cobalt silver mines, which produced until the 1950s, eventually produced over 460 million ounces of silver, depositing the modern equivalent of $2 billion into the young economy.

If the American Wild West had not been so crime-ridden, the electronic computer might not have developed as rapidly as it did.

The revolutionary method of managing data by machine – cards with holes punched in them that could be read automatically – was inspired by an elaborate and ultimately unworkable crime reduction scheme on long-distance railways. The scheme failed, but the method it tried to use caught the imagination of an inventor who recognised it was the way he had been looking for, for his mechanical tabulating device that was to be the foundation of the modern computer.

The original problem to be solved was the frequent robberies on cross-country trains. Robbers masqueraded as passengers until the train was out in the wilds, and then held up their fellow passengers. An ingenious scheme was proposed to gain identification of the thieves by coding every rail ticket purchased with the physical characteristics of the passenger buying it. After a robbery, the details of all the remaining passengers would be matched against the master record, and those missing would have identified themselves as the culprits and the authorities would have physical descriptions.

The identifying marks – shape of features, colour of hair, eyes, etc. – would be marked on the ticket by the punching of holes next to each descriptor printed on the ticket.

The scheme was never widely practised, but the marking method was an inspiration to an inventor looking for a way to develop a machine that could count, and count quickly – for the American national census of 1890.

Herman Hollerith, a Census Bureau statistician and technician, came across the defunct scheme and realised the hole-punching approach could be used for transferring information from census forms on to cards that could then be read electronically and counted by machine.

He patented the world's first electronic tabulator in 1889 and used it for the following year's census which enabled the count to be completed in six weeks, compared with the previous census in 1880 which had taken three times as long, even though the population of the country was then only 50 million and had since increased to 60 million.

So successful was Hollerith's machine that he set up his own Tabulating Machine Company in 1896 that, in 1911, became one of the firms that formed International Business Machines – IBM, the modern computer giant. Until floppy disks arrived in the 1980s, all computer data inputting was done by Hollerith's method of punched cards – the railway crime prevention scheme that failed.

The introduction of the news magazine programme on early evening British television came about because of the abolition of a bizarre practice that was followed by the BBC and ITV from the inception of daily broadcasting. Both shut down at 6pm to allow parents to get their children off to bed more easily. The stations recommenced for the evening at 7pm.

The ending of the 'toddlers truce' in 1957 meant stations suddenly had a long gap to fill. It heralded the onset of a tradition of British television that lasted well into the era of satellite TV. Beginning with *Tonight* and later *Nationwide* in the 1970s, it introduced some of television's most famous faces to the screen, the likes of Alan Whicker, Cliff Michelmore, Frank Bough and Sue Lawley.

Even today, the theme of a features-style, human interest programme to follow the main evening news endures, but few would know the curious origins that go back to a time when television exercised a degree of social responsibility that looks positively antique today.

7

Artistic Strokes (of Luck)

One of the greatest works of early English literature, Sir Thomas Malory's tale of the Arthurian legends, *Morte D'Arthur,* was written largely or entirely while Malory was in prison between 1468 and 1470 for plotting against the king.

Samuel Taylor Coleridge's most famous poem, *Kubla Khan* ('In Xanadu did Kubla Khan a stately pleasure-dome decree') is only 54 lines long. It should have been over 300, but a knock at the door ruined it.

The poem was conceived by Coleridge in a medicine-induced dream while he was recovering from illness in the summer of 1797, in a lonely farmhouse on Exmoor. He had fallen into a deep sleep of over three hours from which he woke with a vivid sense of a complete composition in his head. Taking pen and paper, according to his own account, he was confident that he 'could not have composed less than from two to three hundred lines.'

He rapidly produced what is now the poem, but was then interrupted by a visitor from the neighbouring village who detained him in conversation for over an hour. Unfortunately, when he returned to his room and tried to take up where he had left off, he found that he had forgotten the rest of poem.

Charles Dodgson ('Lewis Carroll') did not intend to write out his _Alice's Adventures in Wonderland_. The Oxford college lecturer had told it as a story to amuse the three young sisters he took on a three-mile boat ride on the Thames near the university on a summer afternoon in 1862. One of them, Alice Liddell, daughter of the Dean of Dodgson's college, implored him to write it down. He spent the whole of a night writing what he could remember of the tale. He presented a handwritten and hand-illustrated version of the book to Alice, naming her as the central figure, as a Christmas present two years later. Those who saw it pressured him to have it published. It came out to wide acclaim the following year. So successful was it that he followed it up with _Through the Looking Glass_ in 1872.

Henry Rider Haggard only wrote his classic and best-selling novel, _King Solomon's Mines_, in response to a bet from his brother. The 29-year-old bored lawyer, who had just one book to his name – for which he had had to pay £50 to be published and only sold 150 copies – was asked in 1885 for his opinion of Robert Louis Stevenson's recently published adventure, _Treasure Island_. Haggard said he could produce a better story, and completed his riposte in just six weeks. It was published in the same year as _Treasure Island_, was an instant success and those six weeks transformed Rider Haggard's life.

He nearly did not benefit from the remarkable success. As a novice who needed the money, he initially accepted the publisher's offer of a flat fee of £100 for the copyright. While the editor was out of the room, his clerk suggested Haggard should take the alternative of a percentage royalty. He changed his mind, to his everlasting good fortune.

Agatha Christie had no plans to become a writer. She had had no schooling as a child – her mother had an idiosyncratic belief that no child should look at a book before the age of eight – and even into her 20s harboured no desire to become an author. In her autobiography, she declared, 'It never even entered my head.'

It was her work as an assistant in a chemist's dispensary in Torquay in her mid-20s that changed her career. There, she began to nurture her fascination with poison, which would inspire many of her plots. Her first attempt at writing, *The Mysterious Affair at Styles*, was rejected by six publishers. It was eventually brought out in 1920, to little notice, when she was already 30 years old.

Ironically, although she was excruciatingly shy and detested publicity, it was her famed disappearance for 10 days in 1926 (now believed to have been a nervous breakdown on discovering her husband was having an affair) that brought her the national attention that elevated her to celebrity status.

At least one novel a year appeared from the 1930s through to the 1950s. She would end up writing 78 crime novels, 150 short stories, 6 non-fiction works and 20 plays. Her estimated sales throughout the world are some 2 billion copies, in over 100 languages.

Thirty years after her death, she was still selling a million paperback copies in Britain every year.

Fyodor Dostoevsky, one of Russian literature's greatest figures, was nearly executed when he was 28 after he had written just two, now forgotten, novels. The author of *Crime and Punishment, The Idiot* and *The Brothers Karamazov*, which he produced between 1861 and 1880 (between his 40s and 60s), was a political activist in St Petersburg in his younger days and found himself arrested with five others in 1849.

They were all sentenced to death by firing squad. On 22 December, the execution was under way – the first three, not including Dostoevsky, had already been tied to pillars in readiness – when a royal reprieve arrived. They were instead despatched to Siberia for four years' hard labour.

Accounts disagree whether in fact it was simply a mock execution laid on to scare the young minds. Whichever it was, the trauma of the episode had a lasting creative effect on Dostoevsky, which emerged later in his mature novels whose dark themes were commonly built around intense human suffering and despair.

We are left with the conclusion that either way, this narrowly avoided event was pivotal for Dostoevsky. If the execution was real, he was lucky to have escaped; if it was a set-up, it seems that it left on him a vital and lasting impression that guided the best of his writings.

Gravesend in Kent launched the career of one of Russia's greatest composers and all because a cargo ship had an unplanned delay in the port.

Nikolay Rimsky-Korsakov was a young midshipman aboard the Russian clipper, the *Almaz*, which had left St Petersburg in November 1862 on a two-and-a-half year trading cruise across the Atlantic and around the Mediterranean.

The ship had had no plans to come to Britain. It intended to head straight for New York but a couple of days out from St Petersburg the captain decided that the *Almaz*, which had just had an extensive refit, had not been given large enough masts to make a sufficiently fast crossing of the Atlantic. Opting to have them replaced in England, he sent an order on ahead and put into Gravesend a few days later. The ship and its crew would spend the next four months in the port and for the young Rimsky-Korsakov it was a period which changed his life for ever.

Just 18 years old at the time, Rimsky-Korsakov had recently graduated from the St Petersburg Naval College, enthusiastically hoping to emulate his brother, 22 years his senior, who had fashioned out a brilliant naval career. Although a talented musician he had had no ambitions in that direction.

He had been an accomplished piano player since the age of six, and while at the Naval College revived his piano lessons and through them had come under the sway of one of the great contemporary composers, Balakirev, who encouraged the youngster to compose music of his own.

Under Balakirev's guidance, Rimsky-Korsakov was attempting to write his first orchestral piece. It was hard going and by early 1862 he just had the slow movement to do. It was then that he graduated from the Naval College and the landmark decision had to be made – to carry on composing or go to sea.

He put to sea. And he might have remained a sailor for the rest of his life had the enforced stop at Gravesend not left him the unbroken four months at this crucial time in his life to devote to finishing his First Symphony.

He posted the last movement back to Balakirev and the great man pronounced it to be the best part of the entire work. Rimsky-Korsakov had composed the entire piece without the aid of a piano, as the ship did not have one. He recalled, however, in his memoirs that he played it once or twice in its entirety at a restaurant in Gravesend, the first audience to hear one of his works.

When the *Almaz* sailed from the Thames at the end of February 1863, the die was cast for Rimsky-Korsakov. On his return to Russia he took up music full time.

Evelyn Waugh attempted suicide as a 21-year-old, three years before he published his first novel, *Decline and Fall*, which was hugely successful and launched a career which lasted 40 years and produced gems such as the comic war novel *Scoop* and the grand *Brideshead Revisited*.

Waugh decided to drown himself off a deserted beach, but swam into a shoal of stinging jellyfish and, according to his biographer, 'was stung back to reason'.

West Country novelist Thomas Hardy almost did not survive his birth in 1840 because everyone thought he was stillborn. He did not appear to be breathing and was put to one side for dead. The nurse attending the birth only by chance noticed a slight movement that showed the baby was in fact alive.

He lived to be 87 and gave the world 18 novels, including some of the most widely read in English literature.

When he did die, there was controversy over where he should be laid to rest. Public opinion felt him too famous to lie anywhere other than in Poets' Corner in Westminster Abbey, the national shrine. He, however, had left clear instructions to be buried in Stinsford, near his birthplace and next to his parents, grandparents, first wife and sister. A compromise was brokered. His ashes were interred in the Abbey. His heart would be buried in his beloved home county.

The plan agreed, his heart was taken to his sister's house ready for burial. Shortly before, as it lay ready on the kitchen table, the family cat grabbed it and disappeared with it into the woods. Although, simultaneously with the national funeral in Westminster Abbey, a burial ceremony took place on 16 January 1928, at Stinsford, there is uncertainty to this day as to what was in the casket: some say it was buried empty; others that it contained the captured cat which had consumed the heart.

Franz Kafka, now seen as one of the 20th century's most insightful authors, hardly published any work before his death in 1924 aged only 40. He instructed in his will that all his manuscripts be destroyed after his death. He had published only a few short stories. Three major novels were unfinished.

His literary executor, Max Brod, ignored the request and oversaw the publication of the novels, *The Trial*, *The Castle* and *Amerika*. He later rationalised his actions by saying that he had told Kafka he would ignore the instruction. Thus, he maintained, if

Kafka really had wanted them destroyed, he would have chosen another executor.

A clinical depressive for most of his life, Kafka's works deal with the fate of ordinary people trapped in tussles with forces outside their control or understanding. They have come to be seen as literary masterpieces evocatively foreshadowing the totalitarian trends of the 20th century.

Had Kafka's wishes been followed, his name and these seminal works would never have made their entry into the pantheon of modern literature.

One of the most successful novels in publishing history only came about because the author was laid up with an injury.

Gone with the Wind, according to one list the 49th best-selling book ever written with sales of 28 million copies, sold its first million within six months of publication in June 1936, a phenomenal achievement at the height of the Depression. Its author, Atlanta newspaper reporter Margaret Mitchell, only wrote it because she had broken her ankle. When it refused to heal properly, she had had to give up her job and stay at home.

It was the only book she ever published.

The 1939 film has been recognised as the highest-grossing movie of all time. An estimate in 1996 put its earnings, adjusted for inflation and relative costs of tickets, at £1.7 billion. By comparison, the next best was *The Sound of Music* with a relatively paltry £629 million. But the film nearly wasn't made.

All the big three studios, MGM, Twentieth Century-Fox and Warner Brothers, turned it down. It eventually found its way to David O. Selznick. Not even his director, Victor Fleming, had much confidence, warning Selznick that the film would be 'one of the biggest white elephants of all time.'

Literature's most famous spy, James Bond, acquired his name because author Ian Fleming was an avid bird watcher. The real James Bond was a young academic explorer from Philadelphia who became the authority on bird species of the Caribbean. His 1936 treatise on *Birds of the Caribbean* was the first to catalogue the region's birdlife. It was bedtime reading for Fleming, who lived for long stretches of the year in Jamaica.

When he began writing the first Bond novel, *Casino Royale*, in 1952, Fleming was searching for a name. He lighted upon Bond's book. 'It struck me that this name – brief, unromantic and yet very masculine – was just what I needed, and so James Bond II was born.'

Another curious origin in the Bond books was the naming of *M*, the Head of the British Secret Service from whom Bond took all his orders. His (or, as in recent films, her) identity is never revealed any further. Fleming derived the idea of the name from his childhood practice of always referring to his mother as 'M'.

The only draft of Dylan Thomas' masterpiece radio play, *Under Milk Wood*, had to be retrieved from a London pub after Thomas, a notorious alcoholic, lost it during a pub crawl. He had no idea which hostelry he had left it in and a BBC producer had to scour the city before closing time to avoid a cleaner unwittingly consigning it to the rubbish sack.

Author V. S. Naipaul was sacked early in his career as the Cement and Concrete Association's press officer. They said he couldn't write. He went on to win the Nobel Prize for Literature in 2001.

Rudyard Kipling might have pursued a relatively anonymous career as a journalist in the United States had it not been for the editor of the *San Francisco Examiner*, where he was briefly employed, sacking the future novelist, poet and epitomiser of late Victorian imperialism with the advice, 'I'm sorry, Mr Kipling, but you just don't know how to use the English language.'

Sir William Walton, one of England greatest composers, and who provided music for the 1937 and 1953 coronations, failed his final music exam.

After spending years fruitlessly trying to develop the plot of a novel to illustrate man's essential double nature, Robert Louis Stevenson dreamt the storyline of *The Strange Case of Dr Jekyll and Mr Hyde* in one night in 1886. He completed the manuscript within six weeks, and when published later that year, it was an instant success.

The cartoonists who created *Superman* had their idea turned down by New York publishers for four years. Twenty-year-old Jerry Siegel from Cleveland, Ohio, came up with the character in 1934 during a sleepless night when he visualised the entire Superman legend. An old high school friend, Joe Shuster, drew the character.

Their first attempts to interest publishers received the response that Superman was 'too fantastic for our readers.' It was eventually accepted in 1938 when DC Comics were developing a new comic book. Siegel and Shuster were paid $130 between them for the rights, and they worked from then on strictly as freelance contributors.

They later spent over 30 years in litigation trying to secure a better deal as the popularity of Superman took off. Eventually Siegel had to take a job as a mail clerk and Shuster as a messenger to make ends meet. By the end of his life, Siegel said that just the sight of a *Superman* comic book made him almost physically sick. He died in 1996. Shuster predeceased him in 1992.

Among other literary works which might never have seen the light of publication had it not been for the extraordinary perseverance of their authors are:

- Theodor Geisel, who as **Dr Seuss** was one of the most published children's authors of the 20th century (he produced 47 books which sold over 100 million copies in 18 languages), had his first story, *And To Think That I Saw It On Mulberry Street,* rejected by more than 20 publishers (he claimed 28, other sources say 23). After leaving the last one, he bumped into an old college friend on Madison Avenue in New York who happened to be children's editor for Vanguard Publishers. He took a look and 20 minutes later Geisel had his first contract.
- The original novel ***M*A*S*H*** took seven years to write and was rejected by 21 publishers before it came out in 1968. It later became one of the most successful television productions in history.
- ***Lorna Doone***, Richard Doddridge Blackmore's dark tale of romance, had been rejected by 18 publishers and flopped in 1869 when it was released as a three-part edition. It succeeded when it was reproduced in a single volume two years later and has never been out of print since.
- Beatrix Potter's first story, ***The Tale of Peter the Rabbit***, was self-produced after seven publishers had turned it down. It was the first of 22 such tales that eventually became some of the best-selling English children's stories of all time.
- Richard Adams' ***Watership Down***, the cult fable about the lives of rabbits, was one of the quickest books to sell a million copies when it was published in 1972 and has sold over 50 million worldwide. It was initially rejected by 13 publishers, including one who wrote Adams a three-page rejection letter complaining

that the book was too long. He, however, refused all suggestions to shorten it.

- Cited in his obituary as one of the most prolific novelists of all time, British crime writer **John Creasey**, who died in 1973 at the age of 64, was credited with 560 novels under more than 28 pseudonyms. He often wrote a full-length book in a week. It did not start out as auspiciously. By the age of 19 he had accumulated 743 publishers' rejections, said to be a world record.

Hollywood originated as a centre for film production because of the toss of a coin. A New Jersey production company, Centaur, was looking for a better location for film making in 1911 instead of trying to recreate expensive background scenery in the American northeast.

Centaur's two partners disagreed on where the best site was. Al Christie, chief director, wanted California as he aimed to make westerns. David Horsley, the owner, wanted Florida, which at that time was backward, undeveloped, remote but closer. He agreed to abide by the decision of a coin toss, which Christie won. Centaur set up on Sunset Boulevard, the first film studio to set up in southern California,

Within a year, 15 other small studios had opted for the area too, drawn mainly by the variety of natural landscapes of the area and the all-year sun essential for uninterrupted work.

The first words heard in the first talkie were accidental. Al Jolson's 'Wait a minute! Wait a minute! You ain't heard nothing yet,' in *The Jazz Singer* were not part of the script and not intended to be heard. They were accidentally recorded when Jolson called to a stagehand on the set, and the director decided to keep them in.

The origin of the celebrated catchphrase in the 1930s Tarzan movies, 'Me, Tarzan' is said to have come from the astonished reaction of former Olympic gold medal swimmer Johnny Weissmuller when asked by the MGM studios to take a screen test for the part. He exclaimed, 'Me? Tarzan?'

He had gone to the studio to see Clark Gable. The only way he found to gain entry to the film lot was to join a queue for hopefuls auditioning for Tarzan. He was asked to test and got the part.

A scene in the first Indiana Jones film, *Raiders of the Lost Ark*, voted by *Empire* magazine in 1999 as the 'coolest' in cinema history, was not originally in the script and came about only because Harrison Ford, the film's lead, had diarrhoea.

Ford's combat with an Arab swordsman who starts by extravagantly demonstrating his prowess with a display of swinging blades is brought to a sudden end when the archaeologist casually pulls out a gun and shoots him. Stephen Spielberg, the director, had planned a long fight sequence between the pair. Ford was suffering from a stomach bug and asked for the episode to be drastically shortened.

Steven Spielberg's original design of the spacecraft for *Close Encounters of the Third Kind* was scrapped when it did not look right once filming began. No one could think of a right shape. Spielberg was inspired by driving past an oil refinery at night, with its hundreds of tiny lights sparking from the complex of pipes and towers. The spacecraft was suddenly born in front of him.

Twentieth Century-Fox initially wanted to change the title of *Star Wars* as, they maintained, no film with 'star' or 'war' in the title had ever been successful. The film won six Oscars, and has earned an estimated $800 million worldwide.

United Artists had to change the title of a Bond movie when market research showed that fewer than 20 per cent of the American audience understood what one of the words in the title meant.

The title of the 1989 edition of the Bond series was to have been *Licence Revoked*, as the storyline is about 007 having his licence to kill withdrawn on account of his personal obsession with hunting down the killer of a CIA friend's wife. It is the only film of the series where he does not have the licence to kill. But researchers reported that so few Americans knew what 'revoked' meant, that they changed the title to the contradictory *Licence to Kill*.

The song sequence for which *The Wizard of Oz* is now chiefly remembered was initially cut from the film when it was previewed before release. *Over the Rainbow* was judged to slow down the pace of the film. It was restored at the last minute. It went on to win the Oscar for the Best Song in that year's Academy Awards.

Judy Garland starred in film only because of an inter-studio dispute that led to Fox refusing to loan to MGM Shirley Temple, then 11 years old and perfectly suited for the part. Garland, 17, ended up playing the supposedly nine-year-old Dorothy.

The most successful cartoon creations in the history of cinema, cat and mouse duo *Tom and Jerry*, were originally going to be a dog and a fox.

Mickey Mouse was invented only because Walt Disney had carelessly lost the rights to his first major cartoon success, Oswald the Lucky Rabbit, created in 1927. The following year, Disney tried to negotiate with his agent an increased fee for future Oswald cartoons only to discover that Universal wanted a reduction instead and threatened to break the relationship if Disney and his team refused. Disney discovered that legally the studio, not he, owned the rights to Oswald. He refused the deal, lost most of his animation talent who went under contract to the studio and set out on his own. Mickey Mouse was dreamed up immediately afterwards to fill the gap.

Disney may never have emerged as a separate outfit had MGM supremo, Louis Mayer, accepted advice from his staff to hire Disney. Mayer refused after seeing a preview of Mickey Mouse on the grounds that he feared pregnant women would be frightened of a 10-foot high rodent appearing on the screen.

On that bizarre decision, the entire Disney heritage rests.

Bette Davis turned down the role of Scarlett O'Hara in *Gone with the Wind* because she refused to work with Errol Flynn, whom she thought had been booked for the film. He hadn't.

Greer Garson starred in the 1942 wartime classic *Mrs Miniver* only because the first choice, 41-year-old Norma Shearer, had refused the part because she did not want her waning image to be further eroded by playing an ageing mother. Garson was also reluctant as she was just starting out, but had less influence with the studio bosses.

She ended up winning the Best Actress Oscar for the performance, and the success thrust her into the spotlight for a decade.

Humphrey Bogart got his big break with the lead roles in three of Hollywood's most celebrated classics only because George Raft, the most popular actor of his day, refused each of them. He turned down *High Sierra* because he did not want to be portrayed as dying at the end and *The Maltese Falcon* because of the inexperience of the director. According to Hollywood folklore, he turned down *Casablanca* too because 'I don't want to star opposite an unknown Swedish broad.' He later called it the biggest mistake of his life.

Hedy Lamarr turned down the Ingrid Bergman female lead role in *Casablanca* because she would not work with an incomplete script. *Casablanca* became famous in film lore for the writers producing the script in parts as the filming progressed. None of the actors knew how the film ended when they started the shoot: the writers delivered daily scripts to the set.

Bergman had difficulty too – she claimed she did not know whether she would end up going off with Bogart, the old flame, or Paul Henreid (Laszlo), her present husband. 'How can I play the love scenes when I don't know which man I will end up with?' she complained to Howard Koch, one of the scriptwriting team. Koch has said, 'I told her I didn't know either.' He had produced two endings, and did not know himself which one director Michael Curtiz would use.

Boris Karloff secured the role as the monster in *Frankenstein* in 1931 as his features were so craggy the director James Whale thought he looked like his idea of the monster without make-up. His chief rival, Bela Lugosi, is said to have lost the part because he objected to the heavy make-up required and, as an already more established star, he was not attracted to a role whose dialogue consisted only of a series of grunts.

Karloff proved a sensation and went on to make over 50 more films in Hollywood up until the end of the Second World War, including three *Frankenstein* sequels and as *The Mummy*.

Charlton Heston reportedly got the role of Moses in the 1956 remake of *The Ten Commandments* because of his broken nose. Director Cecil B. De Mille noticed his similarity to Michelangelo's statue of Moses that has its nose broken in the same place.

Clark Gable's big break in the 1934 comedy, *It Happened One Night*, came only because his MGM studio boss wanted to punish him. The film's director, Frank Capra, working for the least prominent of the studios, Columbia, had been searching for leads for months and the project was on the verge of collapse. Four leading women had rejected the female lead, and Capra's choice for the male lead had turned it down.

With the film about to die, MGM head Louis Mayer called Columbia boss Harry Cohn asking for a favour. 'We have a bad boy down here I'd like to punish,' Mayer is said to have told him. Being sent from MGM to the lesser studio was akin to Siberian exile for rising stars. Gable was loaned to Columbia and had to take the lead.

It Happened One Night turned out to be a roaring success. At the Oscars that year it became the first film to win all five main awards (Film, Director, Actor, Actress and Screenplay), an achievement not repeated until 1975. Clark Gable was catapulted to fame as a result of his 'punishment'.

Cary Grant was the producers' first choice for the role of James Bond. He declined because he did not want to get ensnared in a series of films. Cubby Broccoli and Harry Saltzman then chose Sean Connery to start with *Dr No* in 1962. Ian Fleming's verdict on the replacement? 'He's not exactly what I had in mind.' It was Connery's first major film lead. He would star in the next seven Bond movies over 21 years.

Sylvester Stallone was the initial choice to star in *Beverly Hills Cop*. When he read the script, however, he demanded the writers put in more action sequences to befit his reputation. The studio objected to the increased budget needed, and looked around for another leading man, and Eddie Murphy got his first full leading role.

Dustin Hoffman, who got his big break as the lead role in *The Graduate* in 1967, was fifth choice for the part. First had been Warren Beatty. He was unavailable, filming *Bonnie and Clyde*. Robert Redford tested but was regarded as too mature. Burt Ward (Robin in *Batman*) chose to commit to that role instead, a choice he openly regretted later as he failed to escape the typecasting and never secured another major cinema part. Hoffman, by contrast, never looked back.

Christopher Reeve was sixth choice to play the lead in *Superman*. Warren Beatty, Robert Redford, Steve McQueen, Paul Newman and James Caan all turned it down. The films grossed over $300 million at the box office, and Reeve starred in three sequels.

Fifties star, Janet Leigh, whose most famous role was as the victim in *Psycho*, and who became the wife of Tony Curtis and mother of actress Jamie Lee Curtis, was given her initial chance in Hollywood only through a lucky break in 1947 when another star, Norma Shearer, came across a photograph of the 19-year-old when holidaying at the Californian ski hotel where Leigh's parents worked. Shearer took the photo back to MGM, which immediately offered her her first part.

Sixties star, Gina Lollobrigida, was approached in the street in Rome in 1946 by film director, Mario Costa. Her initial reaction was to berate him for accosting her. When she stopped insulting him, he offered her a screen test for his film, *Elisir d'Amore.*

Sultry British actress, Susan George, secured her major career break by deception and perseverance. She tried out for the lead role as a teenage schoolgirl opposite Charles Bronson in a 1969 Lolita-style tale, *Twinky.* She was rejected. She returned the next day to rejoin the queue of 300 hopefuls, this time wearing her school uniform and using a different name. She got the part.

Dudley Moore, who shot to Hollywood fame in 1979 as the male lead in *10*, got the part only because George Segal pulled out after filming had started due to a dispute with the director Blake Edwards. According to one account, he felt that Edwards had over-indulged the demands of the second female lead, Julie Andrews – who happened to be married to Edwards.

Mel Gibson secured his first major film part, the lead in *Mad Max,* in 1979, because he had been beaten up the night before the screen test. He had not expected to be seen and only went to accompany a friend who was also auditioning.

His roughed-up appearance from the drunken brawl – a swollen nose and heavy bruising – was exactly what director George Miller was looking for. He was told to return in two weeks, by which time the injuries had healed and he looked so different he was not recognised at first. But the decision to cast him was confirmed.

Silent era star, Fatty Arbuckle, was a plumber called to unblock film mogul Mack Sennett's drain in 1913. As soon as Sennett saw him, he gave him a contract. He went on to become the first actor to be paid more than a million dollars a year.

Other unexpected starts from menial trade beginnings were Clark Gable – a telephone repair engineer who happened to call on an acting coach who took him under her wing; John Wayne – a props removal hand who was spotted by director Raoul Walsh unloading furniture; and Rock Hudson – a postman whose round happened to include an actor's agent who got him his first opening.

Judy Garland got her first contract break in 1935 by accident when a studio hand misheard Louis B. Mayer's instructions. Mayer had just seen both the 13-year-old Garland and 15-year-old Deanna Durbin. 'Sign up that singer – the flat one,' Mayer had ordered. He had been referring to Durbin. The assistant thought he said 'the fat one' and signed up the then dumpy Garland. Mayer used to refer to her as his 'little hunchback'.

Another MGM discovery-by-mistake was Greer Garson whom Mayer went to see while in London on a scouting visit. He was seeking a singer and went to her play *Old Music* thinking it was a musical.

Clark Gable, who had the tag 'King of Hollywood' in his prime in the late 1930s, twice failed his initial screen tests. Studio boss, Jack Warner, thought it had been a waste of time testing him, as he behaved like 'an ape' and would never succeed with 'those huge floppy ears'.

177

James Cagney was on the point of failure in his first film part in 1931 when studio boss, Darryl Zanuck, viewed the rushes of *The Millionaire*. He performed so badly in the scripted parts that Zanuck thought he had made a mistake in hiring him. Then came the ad-lib that won Cagney his career.

When he thought the cameras were no longer running, Cagney had looked towards the director and sneered, 'Who wrote this crappy dialogue anyway?' The tough guy image was perfect, and Zanuck cast him for the studio's next film, *The Public Enemy*, which made him a star.

Marilyn Monroe's provocative bottom-wiggling walk was due to her suffering from weak ankles and bandy legs. She further accentuated her trademark gait by sawing a quarter of an inch off the right heel of all her shoes.

Charles Buchinski is said to owe his stage name to the vagaries of the traffic-light system in Los Angeles. Driving down Hollywood Boulevard, he had to halt when the lights changed to red. He had stopped at the intersection with Bronson Avenue. He liked the sound of it, and Charles Bronson was duly born.

Other famous screen names that were derived by odd chance include:

- **Carol Lombard**, originally Jane Peters, came from the Carroll, Lombardi Pharmacy on New York's Lexington Avenue.
- Lucille Le Sueur, an MGM discovery in 1925, is possibly the only star to have been given her name in a nationwide competition. The studio thought 'Le Sueur' sounded too much like 'sewer'. They ran a contest in a fan magazine and a woman in Albany, New York won $500 for coming up with **Joan Crawford**.

- **Judy Garland**, originally Frances Gumm, was prompted to change her name when the theatre she was appearing at in Chicago billed her as 'Glumm'. She took her new surname from the review page of the local newspaper that was written by Robert Garland, and her first name from a popular song of the moment, 'Judy'.
- **Doris Day**, originally Doris von Kappelloff, was re-christened by a bandleader for whom she had performed 'Day After Day'.
- **John Wayne**, originally Marion Morrison, was given his new screen name by director Raoul Walsh, who was tasked with finding a more masculine branding. An aficionado of the American War of Independence, Walsh chose his hero 'Mad' Anthony Wayne, a general with a fiery, all-American reputation. The studio still did not like Anthony (or Tony), both being thought too effeminate, so they plumped for plain John.
- **Bing Crosby**, originally Harry, acquired his curious moniker from his schoolmates as a child because his favourite reading was a popular comic strip, the *Bingville Bugle*.

  All the **Marx Brothers** also got their names – Groucho, Chico, Harpo and Gummo – from characters in the same comic strip.
- **'Buster' Keaton**, originally Joseph, was tagged by Houdini, a family friend, when he fell down the stairs at the age of six. Houdini witnessed the accident and exclaimed to his parents, 'That was some buster your baby took.'
- **Michael Caine**, originally Maurice Micklewhite, had adopted the screen name Michael Scott but speaking from a telephone box in Leicester Square to his agent, he was told that there was another actor of the same name already around. The agent asked him to think of another name there and then. Micklewhite looked around and saw *The Caine Mutiny* being shown at the Odeon next to him.

A young British actor failed to get his screen chance in 1985 *because* of his name. Mark Lindsay had been chosen by American network NBC after a lengthy search to play murdered Beatles star John Lennon in a television biopic. It was less than five years since Lennon's murder.

The producers then discovered that Lindsay's real name was Mark Chapman – the same name as Lennon's killer. Lindsay had changed his name when he joined the British actors' union as there was already a Mark Chapman in it. NBC simply said it was 'in the best interest of the project' that another actor be cast as John Lennon.

Over 20 years later, Lindsay eventually got to do the part, starring as Lennon in a 2007 version of the tale.

When choosing the names of the seven dwarfs for *Snow White and the Seven Dwarfs*, Disney's first full-length cartoon, over 50 names were considered. Before he settled on Dopey, Grumpy, Doc, Bashful, Sleepy, Sneezy and Happy, it is possible they might have been any from a list which included: Awful, Blabby, Burpy, Chesty, Cranky, Dippy, Dirty, Flabby, Gabby, Gloomy, Hotsy, Puffy, Sniffy, Scrappy, Shifty, Sleazy, Tipsy, Weepy, Wistful, and Woeful.

The cartoon dog, Scooby Doo, got his name by accident when creator Fred Silverman, who was trying to come up with a suitable tag, heard Frank Sinatra singing 'Strangers in the Night' on the radio. Part of the chorus contained the curious line, 'Scooby-dooby-doo'.

Jack Nicholson, when he won the 1975 Best Actor Oscar for *One Flew Over the Cuckoo's Nest,* used his acceptance speech to 'thank my agent of ten years ago who told me I'd never be an actor.'

Irving Berlin had his surname coined for him when the publisher of his first composition, in 1907, 'Marie from Sunny Italy', got it wrong by accident. The 19-year-old Israel Baline saw his name appear as 'I. Berlin' and liked it. He stuck with it.

The song itself had less impact on his future – it is said to have earned him only 37 cents.

In 1952, two British producers bought the film rights to an Agatha Christie story, with only one condition attached – that they had to wait six months after the end of the story's theatre run before they could make the film. Unfortunately for them, the production was her play *The Mousetrap*, which, 56 years on, is still running.

Both the producers have long since died.

The creator of the iconic BBC police drama *Z Cars*, which ran for 799 episodes between 1962 and 1978, got the original idea because he had mumps.

Confined to bed, Troy Kennedy Martin whiled away the time listening in to police patrol messages on his VHF radio. From these, he said, he got a completely different impression of the real lives of police officers than the one coming across from the archetypal 1950s drama, *Dixon of Dock Green*. Built around the patrol car rather than the bobby walking the beat, the show broke new ground in grittiness and pace, and would herald the later offerings of *Softly Softly* and *The Sweeney* (the latter created by his brother, Ian).

The Flowerpot Men, one of the favourites of children's television in the early years of British broadcasting, originated as three short stories for radio in 1951 written by a Yorkshire-born teacher, Hilda Brabban, for her two young brothers who constantly misbehaved, called William and Benjamin. When one of them had been naughty, their mother would shout, 'Was it Bill or was it Ben?', which became one of the catchphrases of the show.

The other curious turn of language that became associated with the pair – 'Flobadob' – was based on what the boys said when one of them broke wind in the bath.

The show turned to television in 1952, but Brabban, having received payment of a guinea for each for her original stories, received none of the royalties from the television version. The designer who created the puppets always claimed that she had never heard of the radio stories.

Scriptwriter Jimmy Perry got the idea for *Dad's Army* in the course of a walk round London's St James's Park in May 1967. He was drawn to the sound of the military band parading out of Buckingham Palace in the Changing of the Guard ceremony. It suddenly recalled in his memory the moment in 1941 when he had been standing in virtually the same spot watching a troop of the newly formed Home Guard also marching in front of the palace.

The memories suddenly came flooding back (Perry had been in his own Home Guard unit in Hertfordshire as a 15-year-old. Most of the characters in the series would be drawn from this experience). He wrote the first episode in its entirety in just three days.

It became one of the BBC's most successful comedy series, running for 80 episodes between 1968 and 1977.

The classic 1970s comedy series, *Fawlty Towers*, would never have been created had the Monty Python team made a different choice of hotel when filming near Torquay in 1972. The one they did stay at, according to John Cleese who scripted the series with his wife Connie Booth, was run 'by the most wonderfully rude man I've ever met. He thought that guests were sent along to annoy him and to prevent him from running the hotel.' The hotelier criticised an American member of the team for having 'American table manners' and threw out of the hotel a briefcase belonging to another for fear it contained a bomb.

In honour of the original inspiration, Cleese placed the fictitious Fawlty Towers in Torquay.

Yes, Minister, the acclaimed political comedy series of the 1980s, was inspired by a single instance of a government minister's hypocrisy 20 years before. The creators got the idea for exposing how ministers and civil servants influenced each other to get their way by the revelation that a Labour MP, Sir Frank Soskice, had signed a petition calling for a posthumous pardon to Timothy Evans, a *cause célèbre* victim of wrongful execution. When Soskice later became home secretary in 1964, he received the very petition he had signed, but in his new position, rejected it.

How easily ministers were beguilingly manipulated by civil servants became the motif of every episode.

Roger Moore got his small screen break in 1962 when Patrick McGoohan turned down the title role in *The Saint*, supposedly because of the character's bachelorhood and womanising, which McGoohan did not think fitted his demeanour. Moore's performance in the seven-year series created a perfect platform for him to be the natural successor to Sean Connery as the big screen Bond.

The Saint also made Volvo famous in Britain. He was to have promoted an iconic British car, the E-Type Jaguar, but the company refused to lend one for the show.

***Bergerac*, one of British television's longest-running detective dramas,** came about only because the BBC's existing crime investigator series, *Shoestring,* ended unexpectedly when the lead actor decided against committing to another series. Trevor Eve, who had played the eponymous hero for two seasons, backed out in 1980, leaving a gap in the scheduling for the following autumn.

In October 1981, John Nettles opened in what was intended as a stopgap show while a longer-term replacement was mapped out. The unlikely and plot-limiting setting of tiny Jersey seemed to hold out little prospect for a prolonged run. In the event, it lasted for 10 years and nearly 90 episodes.

***Black Adder* was nearly axed after the first series** as it was not felt to have 'enough laughs to the pound', according to Michael Grade, responsible for commissioning the show at the BBC. It only got a second series by agreeing to drop the expensive outdoor filming and opt for the cheaper studio-based format. The three series that followed made the show one of the BBC's most popular outputs of the 1980s.

***Dr Who* was originally conceived in 1962 as a family educational programme**, using the time travel theme to explain world history and possible futures. Creator Sydney Newman envisaged the Doctor's companions – his granddaughter and two schoolteachers – as the vehicles for the educational dimension. His instructions to the production team were very clear: 'No cheap-jack bug-eyed monsters.'

The arrival of Terry Nation early on as a scriptwriter, and his vision of the Doctor visiting alien worlds, led to the Daleks being introduced when the second story began. The Dalek phenomenon was so popular with audiences that plots took off in an entirely different direction, the one for which the show is better known and which has been the secret of its success over 45 years to the present day.

Newman's original vision of historical settings were given airings in the first two series then dropped completely. Newman ceased to influence the show, and in 1967 left the BBC entirely and returned to his native Canada. He later acknowledged that 'the series became famous, as the world knows, because of the Daleks, the bug-eyed monsters I never wanted.'

Diana Rigg's character of Emma Peel, the catsuited partner of debonair John Steed in the 1960s cult series, *The Avengers*, was so named because she was cast as the show's 'M (man)-appeal'.

Watching the BBC's 1976 historical drama of the Roman Empire, *I Claudius*, gave American producer Esther Shapiro the idea for her blockbuster centred on the family rivalries of Denver oil producers, *Dynasty*. She is said to have remarked, 'These Roman families aren't very different from what I see about me.'

The television phenomenon of 1977, *Roots*, which traced the generations of an African slave transported to the American South and which has been credited with sparking the modern vogue for family genealogy, made its colossal impression because, unusually for American TV, ABC screened the entire eight-part series over successive nights. They did so only because they had so little confidence that the show would be watched that they wanted the poor ratings to appear in a single week instead of 'losing' the ratings war for that slot each week for two months.

Ironically, it was the night-after-night format that drew viewers in their millions. The last episode was watched by 80 million people – over a third of the population – a record not surpassed until *Dallas*.

Vincent van Gogh would have been a priest not a painter had he not tried too hard.

He had always believed his vocation was to go into the priesthood. For three years, between the ages of 24 and 27, he tried desperately to gain a place in the theology department at Amsterdam University. When he failed the entrance exams there, he studied for a place at a missionary school near Brussels but failed the entrance course there too. He tried a third time to be a pastor, by becoming a missionary in a small Belgian mining village. It lasted eight months before he was sacked because the school thought his approach was 'overzealous'. Only then did he take up painting. Had any of the three attempts to enter the church succeeded, we would probably never have heard of van Gogh.

James McNeill Whistler went to West Point Military Academy to be a soldier. He put his failure to secure a military career down to not passing a chemistry exam. He once said, 'If silicon were a gas, I would have been a general one day.' Instead, he became one of America's most famous artists.

Pablo Picasso nearly did not survive his birth in 1881 through the negligence of the midwife. Thinking him stillborn, she left him on a table. It was only his uncle, luckily a doctor, who literally breathed life into him by giving him a lungful of air.

The hymn *Silent Night* was composed on Christmas Eve 1818 in the tiny church of St Nicholas in Oberndorf, near Salzburg in Austria, because the organ had broken. The organist, Franz Gruber, made up the tune, which could be sung to a guitar as that was the only other instrument the small congregation had. The priest, Joseph Mohr, composed the words.

They never planned to perpetuate it. It was only when the workman arrived later to repair the organ that they gave him a personal rendition. He liked it so much that he memorised the words and tune and sang them wherever he went. It was not written down or published until 1840.

8

'Unlucky, Sport!'

The name of one of the world's most prestigious horse races, the Derby, was literally coined in advance of its first running in 1780 on Epsom Downs by a toss of a coin. The two progenitors of the idea for a race of three-year-olds of both sexes to determine the best horse of each generation, were racing administrator Sir Charles Bunbury and Edward Stanley, the 12th Earl of Derby. They flipped a coin to see after whom the race should be named. Had the coin landed differently, we would have had the Bunbury Stakes instead.

Ten-pin bowling was invented in the United States as a subterfuge to get round the law banning such sports. The nine-pin version of the game was imported into America by a number of European settlers in the 18th century. By the middle of the 19th century, it had become associated – much like snooker and pool in the 20th – with crime, gambling and disreputable behaviour.

The State of Connecticut banned bowling in 1841, and other states followed their example. So, according to the modern game's tradition, players simply added a pin to make it 10-pin which allowed them to circumvent the letter of the law.

For more than 200 years after the birth of cricket, the standard form of delivering the ball was exactly as the term 'bowling' suggests – underarm as in the game of bowls. The shift along the road to the modern overarm technique was due to Kent's John Willes. He picked up the idea from his sister, whom he roped in to help him practise his batting. That session, around 1822, was to change the face of the sport.

The inspiration came from Christina Willes's poor dress sense. She wore her full-hooped skirt, found she could not deliver the ball underarm so tossed it round-armed instead. Willes found that the way the ball pitched made it much harder to play.

Although Willes was no-balled by umpires at first when he used the technique in matches, by 1828 the game's governing body had allowed round-armed bowling (with the arm allowed to be raised as high as the elbow; and from 1835, as high as the shoulder) and the modern game was born – all because a woman turned up to help in the wrong kind of clothes.

Don Bradman, the greatest batsman cricket has ever seen, entered his last Test innings in August 1948 needing to score just four runs at The Oval to end his career with a Test average of exactly 100. The man who had made 117 first-class centuries and scores of over 200 on 37 occasions, was bowled second ball, for a duck. His record stands in perpetuity on 99.94.

A story circulated that he had been so affected by the reception given to him by the crowd and the England players as he went out to bat that day that his eyesight was dimmed with tears.

Brian Lara broke cricket's iconic highest individual first-class scoring record in June 1994, scoring 501 playing for Warwickshire against Durham, a record that had stood for 35 years. It was the highest score in England for 99 years, and came just 49 days after he had broken the record for the highest Test innings.

It could have been so different – he was actually bowled on 10 by a no-ball from Durham's Andrew Cummins, and wicket keeper Chris Scott dropped a simple catch when he was on just 18.

A potential commercial windfall, however, eluded Lara. His sponsors, a clothing company, had already begun developing a *375s* brand after his Test score. They were flummoxed over *501s* as commercial rivals, Levi Strauss, made *501* jeans. A company spokesman said, 'If he had made 502, it would have saved us an awful lot of hassle.'

It might have been a different record Lara was aiming for had the then record holder's feat not occurred in even stranger circumstances. Hanif Mohammad, playing for Karachi against Bahawalpur in January 1959, having already well surpassed Bradman's existing world record of 452, had amassed, according to the scoreboard, 496 – with two minutes of the day's session left. Off the last ball of the day's penultimate over, he went for a single to keep strike in order to go for the 500 mark in the final over. He was run out.

He returned to the pavilion to discover that the scoreboard had been wrong. He had in fact been on 499 and had been running for his unique target. Would he have done so had he known his true score…?

Golfer Roberto de Vicenzo, then reigning British Open champion, missed ending the 1968 US Masters as joint leader because he signed his scorecard without checking it. His playing partner had wrongly scored his penultimate hole a four instead of a three. The extra stroke meant he finished second – by one stroke, and denied the chance of a play-off for the title. According to the rules of golf, having signed the card there was no possibility of rectifying the mistake.

It also happened to be his 45th birthday.

The first televised maximum 147 break at snooker was achieved by Steve Davis at Oldham in 1982. It should have been three years earlier. At Slough, also in a televised tournament, John Spencer achieved the feat – except that at the moment he did it, owing to a union ruling, the cameraman for Thames Television was on his statutory lunch break. The exploit went unrecorded.

Rubbing salt into the wound, Davis's effort three years later was in a match against…Spencer.

English tennis player Tony Pickard lost an ill-tempered tie at the 1963 Italian Open against New Zealander, Ian Crookenden. His mood was not improved at a crucial game point. Pickard's opponent fired his return nine inches over the baseline but the shot was not ruled out as the linesman was not watching – he had turned away, and was leaning across a fence to buy an ice cream. Crookenden won the point and went on to win the match.

Baron Pierre de Coubertin, founder of the modern Olympics, was inspired in his cause to re-establish the Games from a deep-seated personal drive. But contrary to what you might think, the cause had nothing to do with fostering international harmony and competition in friendship. Far from it. The origin of the Games lay in losing a war 25 years earlier.

De Coubertin became passionate about the Games because he saw it as a way to instil back into young people the martial skills that had been so lacking when France had suffered a crushing defeat by the rising nation of Germany in 1871. The point of the Games in his view was to reverse the general culture of weakness amongst modern man and provide a means for building a stronger nation better able to fight its enemies.

It was also men only. He refused to contemplate women athletes: 'Their role should be, as in the old tournaments, to crown the winners,' he said shortly, after founding the International Olympic Committee in 1894. There would be no official women participants at the first modern Games in 1896 – although there was a single unofficial competitor in the marathon, but she had to run it solo, separate from the men, and on the day after the men's event. She was even refused entry into the stadium to finish the 'race'. No women's track and field events took place for 32 years, until Amsterdam in 1928. After a public outcry over the exhaustion of competitors in the 800m there, the organisers banned all women's races longer than half a lap until 1960.

The hosting of an Olympic Games brings national pride and a permanent place in history. In one case – Montreal in 1976 – it also brought a spectacular financial debt that kept the city on the brink of bankruptcy for 20 years. The legacy from bad management, corruption and labour unrest was a deficit of $US1.2 billion (about $5 billion in current values). The city imposed a Special Olympic Tax on residents for two decades to help pay off the debt, and the Quebec provincial government introduced a tobacco tax to help. The stadium was finally fully paid for on 30 June 2006 – 30 years after the Games.

Ironically, Montreal could have been spared the grief had an audacious plan by American President Richard Nixon to win the Games for the United States succeeded. In the 1970 bidding war to select the venue, Los Angeles and Moscow were the other cities competing. Nixon was desperate to hold the Games, which would coincide with the America Bicentennial, and to thwart the Soviets at the height of the Cold War. It emerged from declassified papers in 2000 that Nixon wanted to offer a piece of Moon rock as a sweetener to each of the 72 members of the International Olympic Committee who would make the selection. The US State

Department objected as they decreed that the precious rock should only be given to heads of state as symbols of gifts to all the people of a particular nation and not an individual.

So Montreal won easily…to their eventual financial grief.

The unusual length of the Olympic Marathon – 26 miles, 385 yards originates from the London Games of 1908 and a children's birthday party.

The standard distance for the race had been a straight 26 miles. The London race was to start at Windsor Castle. A daughter of Princess Mary was having a birthday party, so the race was organised to start directly under the windows of the nursery. When officials measured, they discovered that the race would now end on the side of the White City stadium furthest from the royal party there. So they extended the race by the requisite yardage to bring the finishing line directly in front of the VIP box. Every marathon has been that precise length ever since.

French discus thrower, Jules Noël, lost the Los Angeles Olympic gold medal in 1932 because all the umpires were watching another event when he made his winning throw.

On his fourth attempt out of six, Noël's throw appeared to spectators to land beyond the mark of American John Anderson, whose throw would eventually prove to be the winning length. Unluckily for Noël, at that moment all the officials had turned their attention to a tense pole vault competition nearby. Every one missed where Noël's discus had landed.

Noël was awarded an extra throw in compensation, but none of his remaining attempts got anywhere near Anderson again. Even more galling, Noël did not even manage a medal place, finishing fourth – by a mere 4 inches in throws of over 150ft.

Similar misfortune struck South African athlete, Johannes Coleman, in the 1938 Natal marathon. He returned to the stadium in Pietermaritzburg at the end of the race confident of setting a new world record. By his measure, he was over three minutes inside the record time of 2hrs 26mins.

He crossed the line only to find that the timekeeper was having a cup of tea in the refreshment block. The official effusively apologised – none of the runners, he said, had been expected back so early. Coleman's time could not be verified, and his world record run was consigned to oblivion. It was the peak of Coleman's career. Although an Empire Games gold medal winner that year, he never again managed to get close to breaking the world record.

The 1900 Olympic pole vault competition in Paris was decided through indecision by track officials. Two of the leading American entrants objected to the event being held on a Sunday. Officials agreed to a postponement, and the potential medal winners departed. Then the officials changed their mind, and ordered the competition to go ahead as scheduled. It took place with the athletes who still happened to be around which included, by fortune, three entrants who had just finished competing in the high jump. One of those, the American Irving Baxter won against a much diminished opposition. Both of his colleagues who missed out would go on to beat him in the subsequent American national championships in the following two years, both with jumps five inches higher than Baxter's medal winning performance.

At the Athens Olympics in 2004, Korean 400 metres freestyle swimmer, Park Tae-Hwan, lost his footing as he mounted his block for his heat, fell into the pool and was disqualified for making a false start. It was his only event. His Olympics was over in less than a second.

An even shorter record for participation was achieved by athlete Wym Essajas, Surinam's first ever competitor, at the 1960 Games in Rome. An entrant in the 800 metres, he was told that the event's heats would be held on an afternoon. That was wrong information. When he turned up, he discovered the heats had been run that morning, and that he had been disqualified for not turning up. He returned home without even competing.

From shortest participation to longest: the semi-final of the 1912 Greco-Roman wrestling competition lasted over 11 hours, the longest in Olympic history, before Estonian Martin Klein beat Finn Alfred Asikainen. The bout was fought for the most part under a blazing sun. Klein was so exhausted he could not fight the final, having to give up the gold medal by default.

At Seoul in 1988, the South Pacific nation of Vanuatu had its first ever Olympic Games competitor disqualified before he even started. Eduard Paululum, a bantamweight boxer, ate a large breakfast on the day of his first-round fight and weighed in a pound over the 119-and-a-half-pound limit. He went home never having thrown a punch in anger.

At the 1936 Berlin lightweight boxing tournament, South African Thomas Hamilton-Brown was robbed of his Olympic dream by a referee's error and an eating binge. He had thought he had lost his opening bout when the judges split 2–1 against him. It was later discovered that one of them had got his scores round the wrong way for the boxers and that Hamilton-Brown was actually the winner. By the time his coach had caught up with him, Hamilton-Brown, who had struggled to meet the 9st 9lb limit, had gone on a comfort-eating binge and put on five pounds. Despite a night of desperate weight loss activity, when he turned up for the second round the following day he was unable to meet the limit and was disqualified.

Soviet cyclist, Eduard Rapp, one of the favourites for the 1976 Montreal 1,000 metres time trial, realised he had jumped the starter's gun at the start of his race and stopped cycling expecting that the starter would call him back. The officials, however, ruled his start was legal, and then disqualified him…for stopping.

Inept officialdom reached its apogee in the 1912 Stockholm Games when the quality of the tennis tournament was well below the world standard. The organisers had scheduled the event at exactly the same time as Wimbledon.

The Swedish equestrian team at the 1948 London Games missed out on the gold medal because one of its three members wore the wrong cap. At the time, the equestrian competitions were only open to military personnel, and officers at that. The third member of the Swedish team, Gehnäll Persson, was spotted by the Head of the International Equestrian Federation, in the dressage stage, wearing the cap of a sergeant, a non-commissioned rank. Sweden was accused of a fake promotion of Persson to enable him to compete in the event, and the team was disqualified. His cap had given him away.

The rumpus led to the abolition of the military qualification rule before the next Games. Sweden, with the same team, and incidentally a properly promoted Persson, nevertheless still won the gold, as did the same team again in 1956.

The Dutch coxed pairs rowing team won the 1900 Paris gold by ditching their cox for being too heavy after losing their first heat and replacing him with a diminutive French schoolboy plucked from the crowd. They won the final, with a string of three French teams behind them, by a fifth of a second in the seven-and-a-half-minute race.

The schoolboy, estimated to be between 7 and 10 years old – the youngest competitor and gold medallist in Olympic history – disappeared back into the crowd and his identity is lost to posterity.

In the US athletics qualifying trials for the 1928 Games, the then world 400 metres record holder, Emerson Spencer, failed to make the national team because he thought he was running in a heat. He timed his run to be just enough to progress into the next round only to be told that he had actually been running in the final selection race. He missed out.

Some never even made it, even though they intended to compete. In the 1908 London Games, the Russian military shooting team sent their entry notification to the authorities, but by the time they arrived the competition was long over. It transpired that they had forgotten to take into account Russia's use of the Julian calendar, which was 12 days behind the Gregorian, which the rest of the world was on.

They therefore arrived for their event nearly two weeks late.

The year before the 1936 Olympics, Eulace Peacock had beaten compatriot Jesse Owens in the 100 metres on three of their five encounters, and beaten him in the long jump at the American national championships. A hamstring injury kept him from competing in the Olympic trials. It was Owens who went on to

197

achieve immortality by winning gold in both events (and two others) in Berlin.

Some acts of sportsmanship ended up costing big time. In the fence-off for the 1932 women's foil gold medal, British fencer Heather Guinness pointed out to the judges two hits that she had conceded but they had not spotted. They turned out to be the margin of victory for her Austrian opponent, Ellen Preis.

In the 1956 javelin final in Melbourne, Russian Viktor Tsibulenko, lying in second place with two throws left in the competition, lent his steel javelin to Norwegian rival Egil Danielson who was then languishing back in sixth. Danielson proceeded to throw a world record distance and won the gold by an astonishing margin of nearly 19 feet from the silver medallist. Tsibulenko had to be content with bronze, more than 20 feet behind.

The inclusion of synchronised swimming as a medal event in the Olympics at the 1984 Los Angeles Games has always subjected the Olympic movement to a modicum of ridicule. It emerged some years later that the decision had been far from clear cut, and may even not have been legally approved.

It was revealed in 1986 that when the International Olympic Committee decided the issue, it was voted on by show of hands. Monique Berlioux, the director of the Executive Committee and a former Olympic swimmer and strong advocate of synchronised swimming, was in charge of counting. After a rapid assessment of the two factions, she turned to Lord Killanin, the President of the IOC, and confidently declared the vote in favour of inclusion. 'Are you *sure?*' Killanin is reported to have asked. 'Definitely!' replied Berlioux, reportedly, 'with an air of massive certainty'.

Except, she confided in 1986 to *The Times* newspaper, 'I am still not sure…'

The Indian national tennis side had the chance to win its first Davis Cup in 1974, but it decided to forfeit the final against South Africa in protest against the apartheid regime. The two least fancied sides in world tennis reached the final because most of the professional players in the big tennis nations were recovering from a prolonged strike campaign against the tennis authorities over prize money.

India has only managed to reach the final on two other occasions in the 108-year history of the competition (in 1966 and 1987), losing both ties comprehensively to big boys Australia and Sweden respectively.

The 50km cycling race at the 1997 Pan-Arab Games in Beirut had to be officially expunged from the records after the authorities forgot to close the roads for the event. Only four riders managed to complete the course, one of them after being knocked down by a car.

Traffic was so bad that vehicles carrying supervising officials got stuck in jams and were soon way behind the pace. No one could formally vouch that the course had been adhered to by any of the competitors.

Local football side, Coleridge FC from Cambridgeshire, were due to celebrate being recognised by the *Guinness Book of Records* as Britain's cleanest soccer team in 1983, having never had a player booked since they formed in 1954. The weekend before the new edition of the annual was published in October 1983, they had two players cautioned in the same match.

Ed Oliver finished equal first with two other players in the 1940 US Open golf tournament, but was then denied the chance of playing off for the championship when stewards disqualified him – for the offence of starting his round 28 minutes earlier than his appointed time.

An even stranger way to lose a golf championship was Hale Irwin's missed stroke in the 1983 British Open. In his final round he had a one-inch putt to finish off a hole. He went to play it and missed the ball entirely. The 'air shot' cost him a penalty stroke, and it was by that margin of a single shot that Irwin failed to finish in first place.

American boxer Daniel Caruso was psyching himself up at the start of his bout in the Golden Gloves tournament in New York in 1992. He was pummelling himself in the face with his gloves when he delivered to himself one hit too hard. He broke his nose, and doctors ruled he was no longer fit to fight. He had lost even before being introduced to his opponent.

Henry Cooper astonished the boxing world in June 1963 when he floored the supposedly unbeatable Cassius Clay (later Muhammad Ali) at the end of the fourth round of their clash at London's Wembley Stadium. Clay was in serious trouble and, it later emerged, was helped to get through the difficulty by a subterfuge by his trainer.

Angelo Dundee confessed years later that he had deliberately widened a small tear in Clay's glove as the fighter was still recovering so that they were unusable. This led to a delay of several minutes between the rounds while new gloves were brought from the dressing room. The extra time is credited with helping Clay's restoration. He went on to beat Cooper in the next round.

It was Clay's warm-up bout before his challenge on Sonny Liston for the world title. Had he lost against Cooper, his chances of reaching a title challenge might never have materialised.

The United States were on the other end of a cheating claim in their 1967 Davis Cup tennis tie against Ecuador in Guayaquil. It was the Americas Inter-Zone final, and a torridly partisan crowd spurred the home team to a surprising 3–2 victory. The Americans complained most, however, over the antics of a squawking parrot high in the trees overlooking the court. It only seemed to screech when an American was about to serve.

The match turned into a highly charged affair. The Ecuadorean coach broke his leg when he rushed onto the court to celebrate winning the first rubber and tripped trying to jump the net, and crowds outside threw stones onto the American coach throughout the tie. But it was the parrot that was etched in the defeated Americans' memories.

The effects of the turmoil can be seen by the Ecuadoreans' next performance. They played Spain in a more sedate Barcelona and were solidly trounced 5–0.

It's one of America's most famous sporting 'what ifs'. The Chicago Cubs blame their lack of success in the American national baseball league – they have not won the World Series title since 1908 – on a curse inflicted by an angry spectator who tried to bring his goat into the ground in 1945.

William Sianis, a Greek immigrant tavern owner, self-publicist and diehard Cubs fan, wanted to bring his mascot into the fourth game of the 1945 World Series at the club's famous Wrigley Field stadium. He had even bought a ticket for the animal. Ushers refused entry because of the animal's smell. Sianis cursed the club, saying it would never win another World Series. The Cubs were 2–1 up in the series of 7 before the dispute. They won only one more game, and lost 4-3 overall.

Not only have they not won a World Series since, they have failed even to reach the finals in every season to date. (They had reached seven between 1908 and their last in 1945.) It is the longest dry spell in the American game.

One of the most exciting finishes to an American football match was lost to millions of television viewers when the game overran and the broadcaster, in deference to sponsors, started showing a children's film instead.

The game in November 1968 between New York Jets and Oakland Raiders was 42 seconds from the end. New York led 32–29. The NBC channel cut to its evening presentation of *Heidi*. In the final unbelievable seconds, Oakland scored two touchdowns to overturn the result. In American Football folklore, the match is still remembered to this day as 'the Heidi game'.

Had the Tour de France started as it had been intended, it would probably never have survived and become the legendary sports event it is. Henri Desgrange, editor of sports newspaper *L'Auto*, whose idea it was to create the race to boost the circulation of his paper, initially envisaged the event as a 35-day race. When he advertised for racers in early 1903, so few responded to the daunting month-long challenge, that he only got 15 riders signed up. He delayed the starting date from June to July – fixing on the holiday period that the race has occupied ever since – and cut the race to 19 days, again, pretty much the length that has been followed every year.

With the progress of the race pumped up excitedly in the columns of *L'Auto* each day, the Tour drew thousands of people on to the streets as it passed. So many turned out for the final leg in

Paris that the winner had to be taken into the Parc des Princes, where the race ended, by car. The frenzied finish guaranteed that the Tour would be a guaranteed success in following years. It also saved the ailing *L'Auto*, whose circulation doubled as a result of Desgrange's visionary idea.

Red Rum, the greatest Grand National racehorse of all time (three wins and two seconds between 1973 and 1977) was bought in 1972 by trainer Ginger McCain, who was unaware that he had been treated for a form of arthritis. Red Rum had been a relatively uninspiring sprinter, and was already seven years old. Had McCain known of the arthritis, he more than likely would not have given the horse a second chance.

Golfer Jack Ackerman, playing the Bay of Quinte course in Belleville, Ontario, in 1934 scored a hole-in-one after his ball came to rest on the lip of the hole, and a butterfly landed on the ball causing it to drop in.

Rugby player Gaston Vareilles was selected to play for France in an international match against Scotland in 1911. En route to Scotland, he jumped off the team train at a station stop to get a sandwich, was delayed in the queue and when he returned to the platform discovered the train was leaving without him. He missed the match and was never selected for the national side again.

Jack Johnson, who was the first black fighter to hold the world heavyweight boxing title (from 1908-1915), and was at the time the most famous African American on the planet, nearly lost his life at the peak of his celebrity status. He planned to travel on the Titanic in 1912 – but was refused passage because of his colour.

The brash feeling of self-importance of young Argentinian motor racing driver, and soon-to-be legend, Juan Fangio, saved him from disaster before he had won any of his five world championships.

Driving in the 1950 Monaco Grand Prix, he approached a notoriously dangerous bend and suddenly became aware that something was wrong. He noticed that the faces of the spectators, which he usually saw as a whitish blur, were all turned away from him. The thought is said to have run through his head, 'If they are not looking at me, they must be looking at something more important.' He braked sharply and as he rounded the corner he discovered that his sense of feeling affronted by being ignored had saved him from smashing into a major pile-up involving most of the field which had blocked the track. He went on to win the race, the first Grand Prix victory of his career.

Four times Olympic medallist and holder of 12 world athletic records, Sebastian Coe once explained the origins of his talent: 'If you lived in Sheffield and were called Sebastian, you had to learn to run fast at a very early age.'

The legendary Bill Shankly applied and was rejected for the manager's post at Bradford Park Avenue in the late 1950s just before he took the job at Liverpool, a club he was to take to three League championships, two runners-up places and two FA Cup wins in 10 years.

Bradford PA had been a respectable Second Division side throughout the previous two decades. Their fortunes were very different after declining Bill Shankly's services, falling to the Fourth Division in 1958 and eventually losing their League status in 1970.

Years later, the then club chairman ruminated, 'It was the biggest mistake any football club ever made. The guy was unbelievable, one of the English game's three outstanding managers, along with Matt Busby and Alex Ferguson. Bradford is a big city and, at the time, was supporting two teams very well. I think Shankly would have made all the difference. We picked the wrong man.'

And what would Liverpool's fate have been had they not had Shankly for that crucial decade, widely regarded as laying the foundations for the unparalleled success that was to come later in the 1970s and 1980s?

Jimmy Adamson would have been the England manager in their 1966 World Cup campaign, but he turned down the offer of the post because he felt he did not have the experience. He had served as assistant to the then manager, Walter Winterbottom, at the 1962 World Cup and was the Football Association's first choice when Winterbottom retired after the competition. Although he had not applied for the post, he was asked to take it in front of the 59 aspirants who had done so.

Instead, Adamson went back to manage the club he spent his whole playing career with, Burnley. And Alf Ramsey became the England manager.

By the time England's greatest footballer, Stanley Matthews, ended his career, he had achieved legendary status. When he made his international debut for England in 1934 it had been just four years after joining Stoke City at the age of 15. Geoffrey Simpson, the *Daily Mail* correspondent, however, was not impressed: 'I saw Matthews play just as moderately in the recent inter-league match, exhibiting the same faults of slowness and hesitation. Perhaps he lacks the big-match temperament.'

Arsenal would have gone out of business inside their first seven years had it not been for an archery competition. When the Football League expanded into two divisions in 1893, the club, founded in 1886, became the first southern outfit to be invited to join. No other side was south of Birmingham.

Travel costs were soon crippling the club, and they got themselves solvent again by holding the archery tournament, which raised the £1,200 that gave them their lifeline.

Liverpool, one of the biggest clubs in England, Europe and the world, owe their existence to a rent dispute involving near neighbours and rivals, Everton.

Everton were the original tenants of the city's famous Anfield ground, playing there from 1884 to 1892. The club then fell into an argument with its landlord, local Member of Parliament John Houlding, about the annual rent. He evicted Everton and in 1892 established his own club, naming it Liverpool.

Had Everton not disputed the rent...

Long teased for being just a two-side (Celtic and Rangers), one city (Glasgow) contest, the shape of Scottish football could have changed radically in the 1930s had the Scottish League taken up an offer from south of the border.

When the League expelled two clubs, Armadale and Bo'ness, during the 1932–33 season (bizarrely for the offence of holding greyhound racing at their stadiums), two English clubs volunteered to take their place. Both were refused. One was border club Berwick Rangers, who eventually made it in two decades later, the other never did: Newcastle United. Then a struggling First Division club, but League champions as recently as 1927, had the northern powerhouse been accepted into the

Scottish fold, the history of the game there might have taken a very different course.

When Chester City football club built its new ground in 1992, it had to configure the layout of the stands to ensure the club officially remained in England. The Deva Stadium straddles the English-Welsh border, and savvy project managers constructed the main stand and club offices on the eastern side of the ground. They are the only part technically in England, but it allows the club to remain a member of the English Football League instead of the Welsh. The entire pitch lies across the border, so all the action during each game actually takes place in Wales.

Cardiff City enjoy the unenviable distinction of being the club to lose the English Football League championship by the closest margin. In the 1923–24 season, they finished on equal points with Huddersfield, but lost out on goal average, their 61 goals for, 34 against record being 0.02 of a goal worse than the champions' 60–33. Cardiff would have been champions had they not missed a penalty in their final match. It would have given them a better average than Huddersfield's – by 0.005 of a goal.

As the League no longer uses goal difference to separate between teams on equal points, Cardiff's record can never be beaten.

Carlisle United hold the record for being pipped by the narrowest margin for any Football League title when they lost out to Gillingham in the Fourth Division Championship in 1963–64 by just 0.019 of a goal. Gillingham had ended the season with two consecutive 1–0 victories and played the last game of the entire division's programme to haul themselves past Carlisle. To add insult to injury, and strengthen the case against using goal difference, Carlisle had scored 113 goals in the season – the highest total of any club in any of the four divisions – conceding 58. By contrast Gillingham had scored just 59, conceding 30. The goal average method was abandoned in 1976.

The British record for a football score in a first-class match – Arbroath's 36–0 thrashing of Bon Accord in a Scottish Cup first round tie in 1885 – was all the result of a misunderstanding. The Scottish Football Association had intended to invite Orion FC from Aberdeen, but sent the letter by mistake to the Orion Cricket Club instead. Whether the cricketers realised the mistake or not isn't clear, but they changed their name to Bon Accord and gave it a go.

Wembley, the home of English football, would never have had a sports stadium built on the site had a plan for a London version of the Eiffel Tower come to fruition.

The area had become established as a leisure venue in the 1880s, reached from the centre of the city by the new Metropolitan Railway line. To boost usage of the line, the flamboyant chairman of the company, Sir Edward Watkin (who had pioneered the first attempt to dig the Channel Tunnel in the early 1880s), proposed in 1889 a plan to build a gigantic four-legged tower similar to the one just being finished in Paris. At 1,150ft, the Watkin Tower would be the tallest in the world, edging out the Eiffel Tower by nearly a hundred feet.

Construction started but when the legs were 200ft high, serious problems were discovered with the ground conditions. The foundations shifted, were ruled unsafe to support such a tower and the project was abandoned. The remnants of the grand scheme stayed until 1907 when they were demolished.

When the government was looking for a site for the 1924 British Empire Exhibition, the centrepiece of which would be a national sports stadium, the cleared and unused Wembley area was a perfect location. Wembley Stadium was built on the site of the Watkin Tower, and put up in just 300 days.

Injuries are all part of the game. But some ailments have had the least expected cause:

- Manchester United goalkeeper **Alex Stepney** shouted so much at his defenders in a match against Birmingham in 1975 that he dislocated his jaw.
- **Darren Barnard**, a Barnsley player, slipped on a puddle of his new puppy's pee on the kitchen floor and damaged knee ligaments. It kept him out of action for five months.
- Bolton striker **Dean Holdsworth** injured himself in October 2000 slipping on grass cuttings after mowing his lawn and straining his groin.
- Spain's first choice goalkeeper, **Santiago Canizares,** missed the entire 2002 World Cup after dropping a bottle of aftershave in his hotel bathroom. It shattered and a piece of glass severed a tendon in his big toe.
- **Alan Wright**, a 5ft 4in former Aston Villa footballer, strained his knee reaching for the accelerator of his new Ferrari. He later swapped it for a Rover.
- Brentford goalkeeper, **Chic Brodie**, had his career ended in 1970 when a sheepdog ran on to the pitch during a match and chased the ball that Brodie was about to pick up. The dog crashed into Brodie, shattering his kneecap. He never played professional football again.
- **Paulo Diogo**, a Swiss footballer, celebrated setting up a goal in 2004 by jumping up at the boundary fence in front of his Servette team's supporters. His ring finger caught in the netting and when he jumped back down, the ring and most of his finger stayed put. Writhing in agony, he was given a yellow card by the referee who thought he was acting. Although the severed finger was found, doctors were unable to reattach it.

- Sevilla player, **Marcos Martin**, was injured during the game against Tenerife in February 1997 and was being taken off the field on a motorised buggy. The driver went too close to the goal and Martin sustained a further injury from whacking his head against the post.

- Non-League player, **Robbie Reinelt**, a Braintree striker, severely gashed his leg in 2001 when the treatment table he was lying on, receiving first aid for a minor injury, collapsed under him. He missed more games because of that injury than he would have done from his original problem.

- **Kevin Kyle**, Sunderland and Scotland striker, ruled himself out of a match in 2006 because of an injury received from feeding his eight-month-old son. Balancing a jug of hot water on his knee to warm up a bottle, he spilt it into his lap and scalded his genitals.

- **Trevor Franklin**, opening batsman for New Zealand, never appeared in the 1986 Test series after being run down by an airport baggage cart shortly after the team had stepped off the plane at Gatwick. He suffered multiple leg fractures and was out of the game for a year and a half. He could never sprint afterwards.

- Golfer **Colin Montgomerie** was so confident that his form had peaked for the 2002 British Open that he was quoted on the eve of the opening round as claiming, 'I should win by five shots.' Going to breakfast at his hotel the next morning, he tripped on a step, hurt his wrist which broke his fall and lasted just seven holes in the competition before having to retire.

- In 1990, Toronto baseball player **Glenallen Hill** injured himself while asleep. Having a morbid fear of spiders, he was having a nightmare of being attacked by them, got out of bed, sleepwalked into a glass table, which shattered, cutting his feet, and then fell down stairs. He suffered severe bruising and missed several games.

- **Adam Eaton**, a Texas Rangers baseball pitcher, stabbed himself in the stomach in 2001 trying to open a DVD wrapping with a knife.

- Trinidadian boxer **Anthony Joseph** broke his leg as he struggled to get up from being knocked down after 86 seconds of his world light middleweight title bout in London in 1996. He twisted his ankle and fell back, fracturing his right leg. He never boxed again.

Billy Jones, a charity fund-raiser planning to crawl around the 38-mile Isle of Man TT motor-racing circuit in 1994, had to abandon his effort after just six miles when he was overcome by the exhaust fumes of his sponsor's car – which was preceding him just two feet ahead.

A charity effort failed at the last minute in 1999 when cyclist Steven Watts neared the end of his 900-mile ride from Land's End to John O'Groats. To celebrate his imminent achievement, he hauled his physiotherapist on to his crossbar to ride the last 500 yards together. They wobbled, both fell off, and Watts fractured his skull – within sight of the finishing line. They were allowed to claim completion of the ride as they were within the city limits of John O'Groats.

9

Crime – Missed Demeanours

The exposure of Dutch art forger Han van Meegeren, who had produced 14 paintings in the style of national master, Vermeer, which had fooled the art world for a decade, came about by sheer luck at the end of the Second World War because one of his productions had been found in the vast collection of art amassed by the captured Nazi Air Minister, Hermann Goering.

In a bizarre twist of fate, van Meegeren was caught out not because his work was discovered to be forged but because he faced the charge of selling a national treasure to the enemy. Goering had kept meticulous records about his art purchases, and all the details of the transaction had fallen into Allied hands.

With a prosecution inevitable, he found he had to confess to forgery to acquit himself of the more shameful allegation of profiting from the Nazis, for which the sentence was death. However, in a further surreal twist, his paintings were so convincing that the court trying him did not believe him. It insisted that he produce another in front of witnesses – which, in six weeks, he did.

He escaped in 1947 with a one-year sentence for obtaining money by deception, and died a few weeks after the end of his trial. He had been trapped in the end by the strange obsession of the Nazi bureaucracy for keeping scrupulous accounts.

Had a secret service official's passport not been out of date, one of the most devastating spy rings to operate in the British government may have been wound up more than a decade earlier than it actually was.

The defection to the Soviet Union in May 1951 of two high-ranking diplomats, Guy Burgess and Donald Maclean, was *the* political scandal of the 1950s in Britain. It was felt to be an even graver affair than the actions of just two men because it was suspected (rightly it later turned out) that they had been tipped off by another communist spy, higher up in the British government. For 12 more years the hunt for the 'third man' went on – with damage to the country's security continuing – until, in 1963, diplomat and MI6 operative, Kim Philby, was unmasked.

Spy author Rupert Allason (aka Nigel West), then a Conservative MP, revealed to parliament in 1989 how close Burgess and Maclean came to being caught on the night of their defection. Burgess was recognised by an emigration officer at Southampton as the pair boarded the ferry to France. The intelligence services were informed and a senior official was dispatched home to get his passport and fly to intercept the ferry when it docked at St Malo in France. It was only when the officer arrived at the airport that he discovered his passport was out of date. He had to return home, mission aborted.

Burgess and Maclean made it to Moscow. Philby continued to operate undercover for another dozen years before he too managed to defect. The man who failed to make the intercept? He later went on to become head of MI5, and eventually receive a knighthood.

Another passport mix-up did for James Earl Ray, the assassin of Martin Luther King, who was eventually caught by British police after fleeing the United States. Two months after the slaying of King in Memphis in April 1968, Ray passed through London's Heathrow airport in transit between Lisbon and

Brussels. While attempting to board the flight to Brussels, he inadvertently showed two passports with different names.

The difference was tiny, but significant. One referred to him as George Ramon Sneyd, the other as George Ramon Sneya. Suspicions naturally aroused, immigration officials examined him further, and a search discovered he was carrying a loaded pistol. He was arrested, his true identity quickly revealed and within six weeks he was extradited back to the United States.

He pleaded guilty to murder and was sentenced to 99 years in jail, where he died 30 years later in April 1998.

One of the most elaborate con tricks of the 1970s was uncovered by complete chance and the tiniest bit of bad luck. John Stonehouse, a sitting Labour MP and former government minister, carried out an extraordinarily well-planned plot in November 1974 to fake his death by drowning while swimming off Miami beach, to escape financial debts and set up a new life with his mistress.

He pitched up in Melbourne, Australia, and began accessing the 36 different bank accounts he had set up in his own and several assumed names. This caused suspicions in the close-knit banking system and police were called in and started to trail him.

They did so because they wrongly believed him to be the missing peer, Lord Lucan who, in an untimely echo for Stonehouse, had also disappeared a fortnight after him after killing his family nanny in a botched attempt to murder his wife (see below).

But one false lead led to uncovering the small mistake that would doom Stonehouse. By chance, the police officer who went to his apartment to investigate, noticed a book of matches in the room. They were from a hotel in Miami, which by coincidence the officer had visited 20 years earlier.

It was that single clue that prompted his arrest a few days later when the officer read of the Stonehouse disappearance.

Stonehouse was tried at the Old Bailey in 1976 with his

mistress and sentenced to seven years. He served three and died in 1988.

Lord Lucan's crime went horribly wrong because of a single change of fortune. His plan to kill his estranged wife in the basement kitchen of their house in London's fashionable Lower Belgrave Street hinged on the nanny having the night off on Thursdays. His wife would be the lone adult in the house and would, he knew, just after 9pm, come down to the kitchen to make her evening cup of tea.

Lucan secreted himself in the kitchen, having taken the light bulb from the socket. When, on cue, he heard footsteps arriving, he beat the woman to death with a length of lead piping.

Unfortunately for Lucan, the victim was not his wife, but the nanny, 29-year-old Sandra Rivett. She had decided not to go out with her boyfriend as usual, but stay at home. He discovered the unwelcome fact when, still assuming the person he had killed was his wife, he heard her calling from an upper room for Sandra. She came downstairs and he attacked her too, but unsuccessfully, allowing her to flee the house and raise the alarm.

Lucan disappeared that night and has never been seen again.

Government papers released in 2005 revealed an elementary error in Scotland Yard's operation to recover Great Train Robber Ronnie Biggs from his hideout in Brazil that enabled him to remain at large for a further 27 years.

Biggs had been on the run since escaping from Wandsworth prison in 1965. In February 1974, the *Daily Express* discovered he was living in Rio de Janeiro and tipped off the Yard. Fearful that news would leak and alert Biggs if they contacted the Brazilian authorities, detectives decided, without telling anyone in either government, to fly directly to Brazil and obtain his arrest.

When Detective Chief Superintendent Jack Slipper arrived at

Copacabana police station, it had to be explained to him that he had no jurisdiction. The attempt was fiercely resented by the Brazilian government, and the publicity Slipper wanted to avoid quickly surfaced.

Ironically, according to the files, had the request been passed through the formal channels, Biggs could have been arrested by Interpol officers in Rio and he would have been handed over to Interpol officers of Scotland Yard 'within a short period with little or no publicity.'

It would be nearly three decades before Biggs returned to Britain, and jail, voluntarily in 2001.

Peter Sutcliffe, the 'Yorkshire Ripper' who killed 13 women between 1975 and 1980, was interviewed 10 times by police between 1978 and his capture over evidence that tied him to the crimes. He would commit four more murders before being caught, and even then his capture was entirely accidental.

Two early pieces of evidence in 1978 – a brand new £5 note found on a victim that narrowed down potential employers, and witness sightings of his car which had been seen on at least seven occasions in the same area of Bradford where some of the victims had worked as prostitutes – were not connected by investigators as different officers were pursuing the different leads.

Hoax letters and a tape recording, supposedly from the killer, in 1979 then sent police off the trail looking for their man in Sunderland rather than Yorkshire, despite strong evidence quickly emerging that all the information in the letters and tape could have been obtained from newspaper reports. The publicity given to the tape led to the number of suspects rising to 17,000. More devastatingly for the investigation, anyone without a Sunderland accent was eliminated from enquiries.

As well as 10 interviews, police would, towards the end, even reject a tip-off from a close associate of Sutcliffe's, directly pointing to him as a likely suspect.

Sutcliffe was eventually caught by a complete stroke of luck. In January 1981, a police patrol in the Sheffield red-light district investigated a car for a minor traffic offence. Sutcliffe, the driver, was interviewed and, having given a false name to begin with, the Ripper Squad were notified. Nevertheless, the squad recommended his release but at the last moment a senior suggested a blood test be taken.

At the same time, the Sheffield officer who had originally picked him up remembered Sutcliffe had gone off 'for a pee' into an alley. When the scene was searched, the hammer and knife that Sutcliffe had stashed in undergrowth was discovered. In the days that had elapsed, any passer-by could have picked them up.

The suspicious weapons, and the results of the blood test – Sutcliffe was B, a type shared by only six per cent of the population – were the breakthrough evidence. His run of extraordinary luck and near misses had come to an end, nearly three years – and four murders – after the evidence had started to point to him.

Within four months of his arrest, Sutcliffe had been tried, convicted and jailed for life.

Later, an even deeper irony emerged. In 1992, Sutcliffe confessed to a 1975 attack made before any of those already attributed to him. The victim had had a clear sight of him and had given police a detailed description. An identikit photograph of him had appeared in the local paper, matching Sutcliffe's particular features, especially the gap in his teeth and his distinctive beard. When the Ripper attacks received publicity later, the victim told police she was convinced that her attacker had been the same man. Police dismissed her claims.

Chance prevailed throughout the Yorkshire Ripper case. It would keep Sutcliffe beyond suspicion for such an inordinate length of time, and then at the end bring police the break that counted.

Britain's most notorious murder case of the 20th century, the conviction of Dr Hawley Harvey Crippen for supposedly killing his wife, would never have come to light but for a series of ill-fated actions on his part. And astonishingly it has since emerged that he may have been innocent of the crime for which he was executed.

Crippen, whose place in history is cemented by being the first criminal to be apprehended through the use of wireless telegraphy, was caught on arrival in Canada after fleeing Britain on a steamship in July 1910. He had taken his mistress Ethel le Neve with him, poorly disguised as a boy. The captain of the *SS Montrose* had become suspicious at the odd-fitting disguise – le Neve's clothes were sizes too big, and the trousers were held up by safety pins – alongside the strange, over-friendly behaviour Crippen was showing to his 'son'.

Crippen's ineptitude at masking the pair's identity was compounded by bad luck: Captain Henry Kendall was an aficionado of modern technology. Earlier in his career, he had actually worked with the radio pioneer, Marconi, in developing ship-to-shore radio. Not surprisingly, then, the *Montrose* under his command had been one of very few ships to be equipped with radio telegraphy (at the time there were just 60 in the whole world). Kendall sent a message back to London and Inspector Dew of Scotland Yard raced out on a faster ship to board the *Montrose* as it arrived in Canadian waters.

Crippen's decision to flee at all had been his undoing. The police, who had been alerted by friends of Crippen's wife who were concerned about her sudden disappearance, had visited Crippen's Holloway home in north London and not seen any evidence of foul play. His story that she had run away with another man seemed plausible. Police were about to drop the case. It was only after Crippen had lost his nerve, and disappeared, that police took further interest and re-investigated his house. They still found nothing on the second inspection, and it took a third before they spotted the loose brickwork in the cellar that led them to discover a mutilated body. Had he stuck it out at home, he might have got away with it.

The headless and limbless torso was never identified as Cora Crippen, but the circumstantial evidence now surrounding the case was sufficient to convict Crippen of murdering his wife. He was tried at the Old Bailey in October 1910 and hanged a month later.

The final twist to the case, however, surfaced only in 2007. Scientists from Michigan State University tracing the DNA of the body found in the Crippen cellar discovered that it could not have been his wife. It did not match the DNA of known relatives of Cora Crippen. The tantalising prospect to emerge was that Crippen was most likely guilty not of murdering his wife but probably of conducting illegal abortions and that this was one which had gone wrong.

Even if his actual crime had been discovered, and in the circumstances of illegal abortions the chances were always going to be slim, the penalty would have been significantly lower than the one he eventually ended up suffering. Crippen's own lack of nerve, and the bad luck of picking the wrong ship to escape on, led to his downfall.

A British murder case was solved with a confession the culprit never needed to have made. Peter Reyn-Bart was accused of murdering his 'wife-of-convenience' whom he had married in 1959 to conceal from his employers that he was homosexual. She had disappeared shortly afterwards.

Over 20 years later, a former associate of Reyn-Bart's told police that he had been told the story of her murder. Police had no evidence and could not act on the tip-off. By coincidence, in May 1983 workers collecting peat found a human skull 300 yards from Reyn-Bart's home in Wilmslow, Cheshire. When confronted by the news, Reyn-Bart confessed to the killing. He was tried, convicted and sentenced to life imprisonment the following December.

By which time, a strange twist of fate had emerged. In October, when the skull was tested, it was found to date from Roman times. It had absolutely no connection with Reyn-Bart's case.

The unluckiest lottery player in Spanish history was arrested for fraud on Christmas Eve 1986 after his plan to make certain money out of the country's annual 'El Gordo' (the 'fat one') national lottery fell to pieces when the least expected and worst possible outcome ensued – he won top prize.

Jacinto Sanchez Zambrano, a bar owner in a poor neighbourhood in Palencia in northern Spain, had bought one of the £130 tickets. His clever wheeze was to then sell shares in it to his customers for £2.60 each, supposedly a fiftieth of the ticket. Except that he sold 250 of them.

He made a small fortune from the sale, recouping £650 for his original outlay. And all would have been perfect except that his ticket won £1.3 million. His 250 ticket holders all assumed they had won over £25,000 each, five times as much as Zambrano would receive. Many went out on spending sprees before the ugly truth dawned.

Two days after the lottery was declared, Zambrano handed himself into the police for his own protection.

A bureaucratic oversight in the chaotic Indian legal system led to a man arrested for the minor offence of fare dodging on a train spending more than 29 years on remand in jail awaiting trial.

The High Court in Patna, in the eastern state of Bihar, ordered the release of Ramchandra Kashiram in January 1982 after discovering that he had been arrested in March 1953 and held in prison ever since, after his papers had been lost.

He had been sent to a second prison shortly after his arrest and had languished for six years awaiting a decision on his fitness to stand trial. In the meantime, his first prison lost all record of his charges or where he was. It was only when his second jail decided in 1981 that he should be returned that the first jail became aware of him again.

He was last heard of preparing for his long-delayed trial in February 1982, supported by two lawyers, neither of whom had even been born when he was first detained. Speaking to reporters, Kashiram said that he would not mind if he was sent back to jail. Having spent two-thirds of his life there, 'I've rather grown to like it.'

The longest incarceration of an untried person is thought to be the 54 years that Indian man Machang Lalung spent in an Assam asylum awaiting assessment for his mental state as to his fitness for trial.

The case was revealed in 2005 when a court in the northeastern Indian state released him after it emerged that the authorities had forgotten about him. Lalung had been arrested in 1951.

Ironically, it appeared that the cause of his plight had been that no one had backed up the complaint for which he had been detained, no charges had actually been filed and thus no record existed of his presence in the system.

An Israeli couple wanting to get married in 1994 were refused permission by a Jewish religious court because of an offence committed by one of their ancestors 2,574 years earlier.

Massud Cohen and his girlfriend, Chochana Hadad, were denied because the Galilee rabbinate had recorded that in 580BC one of Hadad's priest forefathers had married a divorcee, breaking a Jewish ban for the priesthood. The punishment was imposed on all his descendants, and was ruled to apply in this case as Cohen was a divorcee.

221

John Lee, a 20-year-old convicted Victorian murderer, escaped execution in February 1885 because the trapdoor on the scaffold jammed three times in a row as authorities in Exeter jail tried to hang him.

With the rope round Lee's neck, the hangman pulled the release lever but the trapdoor failed to open. He was returned to his cell, the problem apparently remedied, and he was brought out again – for the same thing to happen. When it jammed for the third time, Lee was returned to his cell for good as none of the prison staff was in a state to continue.

All the officials present were so shocked that the execution was cancelled and the Home Secretary petitioned to commute the sentence to life imprisonment. Lee served 22 years before being released in 1907 – the man they couldn't hang.

The world's biggest bank robbery could have been 10 times bigger had it not been for a rainstorm.

The ingenious assault on the Nice branch of the Société Générale bank in July 1976 is thought by French police to have netted close to £50 million. The branch specialised in safety deposit boxes for the discreet and wealthy of the French Riviera. Much of the wealth comprised illicit valuables stashed away out of the reach of the tax authorities or the police. Hence the robbers were confident that there would be few people willing to pressure police too hard to recover the ill-gotten gains.

The gang spent two months tunnelling from the city's sewer system into the basement of the bank directly into the vault. They broke through on a Friday evening after the bank had shut for the weekend, and had until early Monday to rifle the boxes at their leisure.

One small hitch upset the operation. Heavy rain early on threatened their escape. The sewer they had used was the city's storm drain. Its flooding risked them being left marooned inside the bank, so they fled – in rubber dinghies – early, having opened only 317 of the 4,000 deposit boxes.

Despite the curtailment, the amount stolen, while officially declared at a relatively paltry £6 million, was thought by police to be significantly higher, because of the reluctance of many victims to come forward. The unofficial estimate was put at £50 million, which remained the largest heist on record until the £53 million theft from a Securitas cash depository in Britain in 2006. (In 2007, three guards at a bank in war-torn Baghdad are said to have walked off with £146 million from the bank's vaults. The accuracy of the story has never been confirmed.)

British police were taken aback in March 1993 when a drunk looking for a place to sleep for the night unknowingly broke into the headquarters of MI6, the Secret Intelligence Service, in Pimlico, south London. He remained undetected for an hour, and might have stayed so had he not wandered round the corridors instead of bedding down quietly.

Greater Manchester police had to review the convictions of 742 drink-driving offenders in 1989 when it was discovered the police were using swabs already impregnated with alcohol.

Forensic scientists became suspicious when they noticed large discrepancies between the blood sample and the breath test from the same people. It was discovered that someone had decided to change the swabs used when collecting the blood, as those being used were deemed 'too dry'. They had been replaced with swabs already impregnated with four per cent alcohol. The mistake had gone unnoticed for nearly two years.

10

Business – Enterprise and Intuition

'As safe as the Bank of England' was not always the case in its first 50 years. Twice in the half a century since its founding in 1694, the Bank came close to collapse when it faced a run on its reserves. It survived by adopting some small but clever devices to defuse the panic.

In 1720, in the wake of the South Sea Bubble investment scandal, and again in 1745, when Bonnie Prince Charlie's Jacobite rebellion saw invading Scots reach as far south as Derby, the Bank was overwhelmed by panicking investors wanting to withdraw their money. They resorted to tricky wiles.

Clerks were told to work strictly to rule regarding office hours, and pay out only in sixpence coins (then a 40th of a pound). This deliberately slowed down each transaction, with cashiers also using the clamour as a reason for often losing count and having to repeat the slow process of reckoning up the withdrawal.

Large sums were also paid out to friends of the Bank's management who then ostentatiously paid it back in at the cashier's desk to restore confidence. The Bank put its own staff in the crowd too, and got them to deposit the Bank's own money again and again, all the time both restoring faith in the Bank and, more pragmatically, slowing down the chances of real investors actually getting at their money.

The discoverer of the Witwatersrand goldfields in South Africa never realised the value of his find. George Harrison, an Australian prospector, sold his claim in November 1886, four months after he secured it, for just £10. The site, near present day Johannesburg, was found to be the world's richest deposit of gold, with the reef running for a length of 50 miles.

At the time, Harrison was not convinced. He cashed in his luck and disappeared from history's view. He was not heard of again.

In 1993, Chilean futures' trader Pablo Davila, employed by Codelco, the state-owned copper company, pressed the 'buy' button on his computer instead of the 'sell' button. When he realised his mistake, he had already lost $40 million on the trades. So he attempted to recoup his losses, but these trades failed to pay off too. He eventually ended down $207 million – having lost Chile half a per cent of its entire gross national product.

'PG-Tips', the puzzling name of one of Britain's best-selling brands of tea derives from a legal dispute and a trick to try to get round restrictions on false advertising.

Brooke Bond, the makers, sold its tea to chemists and grocers in the 1930s as a medicinal product. It was long thought to be an aid to digestion. Brooke Bond's 'Digestive Tea' was a successful brand. After the Second World War, the Ministry of Food banned the description 'digestive'. In response, Brooke Bond re-branded its tea 'Pre-Gest-Tee', to try to circumvent the restrictions. Delivery parcels were labelled by the letters 'PG' and by the 1950s the name had evolved into 'PG-Tips', from the fact that only the tips of the tea plant were used in the blend.

Forrest Mars, the creator of the Mars Bar and dozens of other world famous sweet brands, only went into the confectionery business after being arrested for a minor offence which led to a chance reunion with his father, whom he had not seen for 15 years, who came to bail his son from the police.

Forrest was, in the early 1920s, studying at the University of California to be a mining engineer. He had been separated from his father since his parents divorced when he was a young child. During his vacations, he worked as a salesman for Camel cigarettes. He was arrested for illegally fly-posting adverts on shop windows in Chicago, and the case was reported in the press. This was seen by his estranged father, who came to bail him out.

That reunion led Forrest to collaborate with his father's sweet business, which was enjoying only modest success. He quickly developed the 'Milky Way' bar and, at the company's British plant in Slough in 1933, the 'Mars Bar'.

Mars died in 1999 a billionaire, having given the world, amongst others, the Snickers bar, M&Ms, Maltesers, Twix and Skittles. And all because of a minor misdemeanour and a chance sighting of a press story.

The spark of insight that led to the development of the home power drill, and arguably launched the modern trend for DIY, came accidentally. Alonzo Decker (of the Baltimore-based Black & Decker Company) began receiving repeated replacement orders for his industrial hand-drills, used by the US military in making armaments during the Second World War. He feared that his product was failing too regularly.

Rather than simply replace the orders, he asked why. He discovered that the problem was not failure, but success. Companies were finding that their female production line workers were taking the pistol-grip drills home at weekends to do home repairs and not returning them.

Black & Decker produced the world's first domestic power drill in 1946. Just four years later they were producing their millionth. The tool that set off the post-war DIY fashion was an instant success. Had Decker just quietly replaced the drills to keep the military happy, he would never have found the phenomenal market just waiting to be tapped.

The modern criss-cross sole of trainers and sports shoes, was inspired by the inventor using his wife's waffle iron to make the first imprint.

Bill Bowerman, founder of the Nike company, pioneered his soles in 1971 after experimenting with the iron after being inspired by the design of his waffles at breakfast. The 'Waffle trainer' was trialled in 1972 and by 1974 had become the best-selling running shoe across America. Nike had revolutionised the market by producing running shoes that were lighter, gave more traction, and were more flexible and more comfortable than any others. Bowerman claimed that his design meant athletes lifted 200 pounds less during a race.

The Saga holiday empire, caterer to the retired holidaymaker, was born from a conversation on a seaside park bench as a hotel owner bemoaned the end of the summer season.

Sidney De Haan, a 30-year-old with a 12-bed hotel in Folkestone, was sitting with his wife as winter beckoned in 1949 after a good, but short, summer. Facing the prospect of having to close for six months, his wife then sparked the idea that was to lead to a revolution in holiday marketing. She pointed out that all around them were people who did not have to go home as they had all the time in the world. She thought the retired ought to be attracted when the peak season holidaymakers had gone home – no crowds, reduced rates, and good company for each other.

The idea went against all the conventional wisdom that the elderly were an impoverished and difficult-to-please market. No travel agent would touch the idea. The De Haans did it all themselves. Sidney worked out the maximum likely comfortable journey time to Folkestone, identified the industrial areas of Yorkshire and County Durham, and went personally to sell the holidays in the towns and villages of the North.

By 1957, De Haan was using rail to transport his passengers by persuading British Rail to provide specially chartered trains and use half-forgotten loops of track to spare his elderly clients having to change trains to cross London. Saga became British Rail's largest passenger customer, a fact BR never advertised.

De Haan launched overseas holidays in the Portuguese Algarve in 1960, one of the first to pioneer foreign holidays. Long-haul trips to the Far East were introduced in 1979 and the first cruise ship started in 1996. When the company was floated on the Stock Exchange in 1978, it was one of the most oversubscribed offerings ever.

The company remains based in Folkestone where it all started.

The Holiday Inn hotel chain was inspired by a Memphis businessman's depressing family holiday in Washington in 1951. Kemmons Wilson discovered that the normal practice of motels was to charge extra for children. He had five. 'My six-dollar room became 16.' This drove him to develop a hotel experience where children could stay for free in their parents' room.

He asked a draughtsman to prepare plans. As he completed his drawings, he happened to be watching the 1942 Bing Crosby movie *Holiday Inn* on television. He drew the name on the top of his plans. Wilson liked it and the name stuck.

The first Holiday Inn opened in Memphis in 1952. Within 15 years it had become the largest hotel chain in the world with more than 300,000 rooms across nearly 2,000 almost identical hotels. The chain was sold in 1989 for $2.2 billion.

Kemmons Wilson is considered the father of the modern inn-keeping industry – and it all stemmed from his own miserable holiday.

A direct offshoot of another ingenious hotel trader is mini-golf. It was invented in 1927 by Garnet Carter, not for its sporting allure but to attract passing drivers to stay at his hotel in Lookout Mountain in Tennessee.

He patented the idea when it became clear that it surpassed in popularity all other diversions available to his guests. Within three years, he had franchised the courses to over 3,000 other establishments.

It proved to be an astonishingly popular, although short-lived phenomenon. In 1930, there were over 1,000 courses in New York and Los Angeles alone. It was so popular that the first to be built on Long Island is said to have repaid its construction costs back in its first day's takings.

However, with the Depression biting, the fad rapidly ebbed away as a self-standing commercial business. It re-emerged in the 1960s, most frequently as a seaside amusement park entertainment.

It would have been Marks and Dewhirst, instead of Marks and Spencer, had Michael Marks won his first choice of partner in 1894.

Marks, a Russian-Polish immigrant who had arrived in Leeds in 1884 as a penniless 25-year-old, became associated with Isaac Dewhirst from the very start of his business career. Dewhirst was the wholesaler from whom Marks bought his goods, which he sold on in the villages around Leeds and then on his street stall in Kirkgate market in the city's commercial centre.

After 10 years, Marks owned a chain of bazaars across Yorkshire and Lancashire. He sought a partner, and his obvious first choice was his trusted supplier, Dewhirst. But Dewhirst turned him down. He recommended instead his own cashier, one Tom Spencer, who was persuaded to buy a £300 half share in the company that became M&S.

229

By 1900, they had 36 Marks and Spencer branches and never looked back. Isaac Dewhirst's name, by contrast, was lost to history. He remains significant, even if not a household name, in the history of M&S. It was he who loaned Marks his first £5 – to buy stock from him to start up the first stall.

The toy car company, Matchbox, which pioneered the pocket-sized miniature car market just after the Second World War, began with a complaint by the daughter of model designer, Jack Odell. In 1950, she told her father that her school had ruled that no one was allowed to have any toy with them that could not fit into a matchbox. Odell then made her a miniature road roller to take to school to show her friends.

That started a flow of models that became the mainstay of boys' toys in the 1950s and 1960s. They continued to be packaged in cartons roughly the size of matchboxes. By 1966, Matchbox cars were the world's biggest-selling brand of die-cast model cars, selling more than 100 million cars a year in over 100 countries with 14 factories in and around London. At their peak, Matchbox were producing a quarter of a million models a week, a rate of more than 1,000 a minute.

A milkshake salesman's curiosity led to a global business phenomenon known as McDonald's. In 1954, Ray Kroc had been asked to supply eight milkshake mixers to a small hamburger restaurant in San Bernardino, California, run by two brothers, Dick and Maurice ('Mac') McDonald. As each machine could mix five shakes at a time, he could not understand why the brothers wanted eight of them.

When he visited the restaurant, he saw why. The McDonalds ran an efficient – and very popular – style of fast food. Their 'Speedee Service' concept was built around having a limited menu, no waiter service, and paper cups with plastic utensils to speed the clean up after a customer had left.

The brothers, who had opened their first outlet in 1940, were quite happy with the business as it was. But Kroc had a vision. Within a year, he had persuaded them to grant him exclusive rights to franchise the brand. He opened his own McDonald's in April 1955, and marketed the brand feverishly. Six years later, the McDonalds sold him the worldwide rights to the name for just $2.7 million. That same year, he grossed $6 million. By the time he died in 1984, the McDonald's corporation was making $8 billion annually.

By 1967, America's 1,000th McDonald's had opened, and there were branches in Canada and Puerto Rico. There are now around 25,000 McDonald's throughout the world. One estimate puts the number of daily customers at 54 million – around 1 per cent of the entire world's population.

The credit card was born as a result of a forgotten wallet at a restaurant in New York in 1949. Businessman Francis McNamara had taken a group of clients to the fashionable Major's Cabin Grill in Manhattan. When it came time to pay, he discovered he had come out without his wallet. He had to ring his wife who dashed over with some cash. McNamara vowed never to find himself in that position again.

He and partner Ralph Schneider invented Diners Club, the world's first credit card. In February 1950, he returned to Major's Cabin Grill and paid for his dinner by card. According to Diners Club, this event is known in the credit card industry as the First Supper.

In the first year, 20,000 people signed up for the card, which was accepted in five major cities of the US by 400 restaurants, 30 hotels and 200 car rental outlets. By 1955, Diners Club had expanded tenfold with 200,000 customers. Until 1961, the card used was cardboard, not plastic. It was to be 1958 before another rival – American Express – came on the scene.

Credit cards reached Britain in 1963, when American Express became available. Britain's own first card, Barclaycard, was launched in 1966. It was the first true credit card. Both Diners Club and American Express were technically charge cards, with the full amount owed having to be paid back every month.

The door-to-door Avon Cosmetics concept was developed by accident because the salesman who founded the company was initially trying to sell books, and was failing.

Twenty-eight-year-old David McConnell – the first 'Avon Lady' – was an encyclopaedia salesman in upstate New York who decided, when sales were trailing off, to offer a small free phial of perfume to anyone allowing him to pitch his products. The scents seemed more popular than the books, so he switched in 1886 and launched his door-to-door 'Avon Calling' approach. He had, unwittingly, tapped a potent market of rural women at a time when getting to larger shops was difficult.

For the first year, he was his own representative. He hired the first female Avon Lady in 1887. By the time of his death in 1937, there were more than 30,000 of them on door-to-door rounds across America. (He adopted the Avon brand as he imagined the area around Suffern, in the countryside just north of New York City where he set up his perfume factory, as looking like Stratford-upon-Avon in Britain.)

Avon arrived in Britain in 1959 and revolutionised home selling. It remains popular, with some 160,000 reps in the UK and nearly five million across the world. The company claims to be the world's biggest direct-sales marketer of cosmetics and beauty products. And all because a man discovered the foot-slogging hard way that his clients really didn't take to books.

B&Q, the do-it-yourself giant, was created in 1969 by Richard Block and David Quayle. It was the first large store specifically aimed at the DIY market in Britain. Block had got the idea from seeing a hypermarket selling domestic tools while working in Belgium. Quayle helped with the market research and the pair set up their shop in a former furniture warehouse in Southampton.

The now famous and recognisable brand name nearly did not happen. The business was nearly called 'Always'. They fixed on B&Q when suppliers started to abbreviate Block and Quayle on sales invoices.

Block left the company in 1976, and Quayle sold the business to Woolworth's four years later.

The curious British product, Worcestershire Sauce, has an equally curious origin, developed by two Worcester chemists – John Lea and William Perrins – in 1835 at the request of a local dignitary, Lord Marcus Sandys, who sought to recreate a fish sauce he had enjoyed when Governor of Bengal. They tried, using the ingredients still used today of vinegar, molasses, anchovies, onions and garlic, but the resulting concoction – perhaps to no one's surprise – was quite obnoxious. It was discarded in a cellar where it stayed forgotten and undisturbed for two years.

When the mixture was rediscovered, it was about to be thrown away when one of the chemists decided to taste it again. Astonishingly, it appeared to have matured in the time like a good wine. It now had a strong aroma and unique taste. Lea and Perrins bought production rights from Lord Sandys and began marketing the original Worcestershire Sauce in 1837. Two years later, a New York importer introduced it into America, and it was so successful that within no time a factory was set up producing the sauce there too.

It has a worldwide cult following. The recipe has remained virtually unchanged for 165 years. In 2008, Worcestershire Sauce was voted in a poll run by a satellite TV food channel as Britain's greatest contribution to world cuisine, beating cheddar cheese, Yorkshire pudding and clotted cream.

The original inspiration for 'Doc Martens' boots comes from a skiing accident and the needs of elderly German ladies.

The original Dr Klaus Maertens, an orthopaedic surgeon from Munich, injured himself on the ski slopes in the Bavarian Alps in 1945 and damaged his foot. Finding regular footwear uncomfortable as it healed, he, along with a former associate from his student days, engineer Herbert Funck, developed the unique air-cushioned sole in 1947. Their principle ingredient was rubber discarded from post-war scrap Luftwaffe aircraft tyres.

They carried the brand name Dr Maertens and were initially designed for the elderly with walking problems. British manufacturers were offered licences to produce them in the UK in the late 1950s, but none saw a commercial prospect – except one: a boot manufacturer, Griggs & Co, who made the standard issue boots for the British Army but who were looking for a new product. They anglicised the name to 'Dr Martens' and produced their first line in 1960. They reached cult status amongst football hooligans and skinheads by the early 1970s.

Puma, the sports company famous for its soccer boots, owes its existence to a misunderstanding between Adolf and Rudolf Dassler, the two brothers who founded a German footwear empire in 1924. Their sibling arguments ended up producing not one but two world-famous brands.

The pair had worked harmoniously until the Second World War producing high-quality shoes, and branching into sports equipment for the 1936 Berlin Olympics. But tensions between them grew as both reacted to the Nazi regime in different ways, the older Rudi being closer to it having been a First World War veteran. The conflict reached breaking point in a bomb shelter during an Allied air raid in 1943 when Adolf and his wife climbed in to find Rudi and his wife already there. According to company legend, Adolf's remark 'Here are the bloody bastards again', which he meant to refer to the Allied bombers, was instead taken by Rudi to be an insult against his family.

The dispute was never healed. In 1948, the brothers split, Adolf ('Adi') Dassler creating Adidas in the following year. Rudi later decided to set up a rival, Puma. They both established factories in the same small Bavarian town of Herzogenaurach, 15 miles north of Nuremburg.

Adidas is now the second-largest sportswear manufacturer in the world. Puma is the second-largest in Europe – after Adidas.

A single, ill-judged speech destroyed the entire business empire of one of Britain's most successful entrepreneurs. Gerald Ratner's infamous joke to 6,000 businessmen at the annual meeting of the Institute of Directors in April 1991 that his jewellery company's products were 'total crap' and that he sold a pair of gold earrings for under £1, which was cheaper than a prawn sandwich 'but probably won't last as long', caused the fortunes of his company to collapse after a public outcry at the mocking insinuation of his customers' poor taste.

The share price of Ratners lost 90 per cent of its value by the end of the year and in early 1992 Ratner stepped down as company chairman. He had seen the value of his business fall from £460 million to just £54 million, and his own stake from £1.5 million to £174,000. The company's balance sheet went from a £112 million profit in 1990 to a £122 million loss a year later. According to *The Times*, 'Never in corporate history have a few foolish words done so much damage.' By 1994, Ratner's name itself disappeared as the holding company dropped the brand because of the continuing marketing difficulties.

In 2003, Ratner made a comeback with an internet-based jewellery business. He was refused permission to use his own name by his former company, which still held the trademark. And instead of the 27,000 employees he had once overseen, his new enterprise boasted a smaller workforce – a staff of just six.

Regarded as the most popular board game of the 20th century, *Monopoly*, invented during the Great Depression by Charles Darrow, an out-of-work Philadelphian, was turned down by Parker Brothers because, in their assessment, it had '52 fundamental playing errors'.

These included the game being too long, the rules being too complicated and there being no clear goal for the players. Despite the force of this rejection, Darrow persevered and began selling handmade versions. Two years later, in 1935, Parker bought out the rights. They sold 20,000 sets in the first year.

Recent research suggests that Darrow was not the original inventor. He took a format that seems based on an earlier game, *The Landlord's Game,* patented by a Maryland social campaigner, Lizzie Magie, in 1903 and 1924, to demonstrate the evils of land monopolisation. To be safe from possible legal difficulties, Parker quietly bought out Magie's patents for $500, and no royalties.

The other great gaming product of the Depression years, *Scrabble*, had a similarly inauspicious start and eventually triumphed only through a single stroke of luck.

Architect Alfred Butts, from upstate New York, created the game in 1931 while out of work. He produced the handmade games in his garage and sold them to neighbours. For over 20 years it remained small-scale and unnoticed. It was not even called *Scrabble*. After toying with *Criss-Cross* and *Lexico*, he called it simply, if bizarrely, *It*.

Butts managed to interest one of his friends, James Brunot, to buy the rights to the game in 1948. He renamed it *Scrabble* from the 'digging' required to select the letters. Two years later he had only sold 8,500 sets – at the rate of a couple of dozen a week – and was on the brink of bankruptcy.

Fortunes changed in a flash when Jack Strauss, chairman of the New York department store Macy's, discovered and played the game while on his annual holiday in 1952. He decided to stock it. Sales skyrocketed to 6,000 sets a week and the 35 workers producing the game could not keep up with demand.

Brunot sold his rights, ensuring that Butts too secured a royalty – 5 cents per set – and while he became a millionaire, Butts received just $50,000 a year at the peak of sales in the 1950s and 1960s. It lasted only until 1974 when his copyright expired. Butts died in 1993.

Experts marvel at one aspect of the game. Butts got all the elements absolutely right first time. The points awarded for each letter have never been changed. Butts decided on their values by counting the number of times each was used on a single front page of the *New York Times*.

A toy salesman who decided to get an early start with his appointments by driving ahead instead of stopping at the hotel he had originally planned, stumbled on the game that he would reinvent and sell to the world as Bingo.

In December 1929, Edwin Lowe, a New Yorker on a selling trip down south, was driving from Atlanta in Georgia to Jacksonville in northern Florida. He passed a roadside carnival and stopped to see why a large crowd had gathered round a table. They were playing something called 'Beano' which offered small prizes for completing lines on a numbered card on sale from the pitchman, who called out the numbers.

The pitchman said he had seen the game in Germany, where it was called 'Lotto'. He had called it Beano because, in the South, beans were readily available to use as markers. Lowe described the crowd as impenetrable. Everyone seemed addicted, and slightly overcome by the tense excitement. One small girl caught Lowe's ear. She was jumping up and down having completed her line and realising she could claim her prize of a small doll. But she shouted not 'beano' but 'B-B-Bingo'.

'I cannot describe the strange sense of elation which that girl's shriek brought to me,' Lowe later wrote. 'I was going to come out with this game – and it was going to be called Bingo!' (Sources disagree whether this episode took place that night, or later when Lowe was trying out the game with friends back in New York.)

What is certain is that Lowe did not make a fortune. He could have tried to copyright the name 'Bingo' but chose not to. He realised that, as the game itself was already in the public domain, trying to restrict competition would have been futile and legally costly. Curiously, he was able to be satisfied that one deserving cause benefited. In the early years, the game was adopted principally by the Catholic Church in America as a money-raising venture for poor parishes.

Index

239

Booth, John Wilkes 55
Bourdillon, Tom
    (mountaineer) 17
Bowling, overarm (cricket),
    origin of 189
Boxing 200–1, 203, 211
Boxing, Olympic 195–6
Bradford Park Avenue FC
    204–5
Bradman, Don 189
Brandywine Creek, Battle of
    72–3
Breathalyser errors 223
British Broadcasting
    Corporation (BBC) 28–9,
    112, 114, 150–1, 154, 158,
    181–5
British Museum 143
Brodie, Chic (footballer) 209
Bronson, Charles 178
Brunel, Marc Isambard
    (inventor) 118
Brzezinski, Zbigniew 112
Bunau-Varilla, Philippe Jean
    13–14
Bunbury, Sir Charles 188
Burger, Reinhold (inventor)
    124
Burgess, Guy 213
Butterfield, Alexander 42
Butts, Alfred (inventor) 236–7

Caan, James 175
Cabinet system (politics)
    19–20

Cagney, James 178
Caine, Michael 179
Calendar, confusion over,
    Olympic Games 197
Callaghan, James (Jim) 30
Canada 12, 156–7
Canizares, Santiago
    (footballer) 209
Cardiff City FC 207
Cardigan, Lord 75–6
Carlisle United FC 207
Carrière, Bob (inventor) 145
Carroll, Lewis 160
Carter, Jimmy 112
Caruso, Daniel (boxer) 200
Carvel, Robert 27–8
Casablanca 173
Cash dispenser, invention of
    147–8
Castro, Fidel 44
Cat's eye, invention of 145–6
Censor, allowance by 31–2
Central Intelligence Agency
    (CIA) 44, 109, 114–5
Chadwick, James (nuclear
    physicist) 131
Chamberlain, Neville 81
Champion (movie horse star)
    152
Charge of the Light Brigade
    75–6
Charity feats, accidents 211
Charles I 48
Chester City FC 207
Chicago Cubs (baseball) 201–2

Chickens, use of in nuclear
weapons 110–11
Chile, loss from speculation
225
China 3
Christie, Agatha 160–1, 181
Churchill, Clementine 62
Churchill, Winston 24–5, 26,
33, 61–3, 79, 89, 98
Cicero (German spy) 87–8
Cigar smoke, influence of 95
Civil War, American 55, 76–8
Civil War, English 48
Civil War, Spanish 79
Civilisation, influence of beer 1
Clarke, Arthur C. 133–4, 151
Clifford, William Kingdon,
Theory of Relativity 126
Clive, Robert 8–9
*Close Encounters of the Third
Kind* 170
Coca-Cola 155
Coe, Sebastian 204
Cold War 13, 44, 45–7, 50–1,
104, 105–115, 128, 192, 213
Coleman, Johannes (athlete)
194
Coleridge FC (Cambs) 199
Coleridge, Samuel Taylor 159
Columbus, Christopher 4
Communism 31–3, 45–7, 63–4
Communist Party of America
38
Computer, development of
157–8

Confession to murder,
unnecessary 219–20
Connery, Sean 174
Conservative Party 25–6, 31
Constantine the Great 2–3
Contact lens, invention of
144–5
Coolidge, Calvin 37
Cooper, Henry 200–1
Cotton gin, invention of 117–8
Courthope, Nathaniel 5
Crawford, Joan 178
Creasey, John 169
Credit card, invention of 231
Cricket 112, 189–90, 210
Crippen, Dr 218–9
Croissant, origin of 156
Crosby, Bing 179
Cuba 44, 105
Cuban Missile Crisis 105–8
Cycling 199, 202–3, 211
Cycling, Olympic 196
Czech crisis (1938) 81

Dad's Army 182
Daily Express 215
Daily Mail 205
Daleks 150–1, 184–5
Dalton, Hugh 27–8
Darrow, Charles (inventor)
236
Darwin, Charles 132–3
Das Kapital 31, 64
Davis, Bette 172
Davis, Jefferson 76

Grauman's Chinese Theatre (Hollywood) 151
Gravesend (Kent) 162–3
Gray, Elisha (inventor) 121–2
Green Eggs and Ham 152
Greene, Sir Hugh 29
Greenland 18
Grenada, 113–4
Grey, Earl 22
Grey, Sir Edward 23
Guinness Book of Records 199
Guinness, Heather (Olympic fencer) 198
Guncotton, invention of 121

Haggard, Henry Rider 160
Hahn, Otto 100
Hamilton-Brown, Thomas (Olympic boxer) 195
Harding, Warren 36–7
Hardy, Thomas 164
Harrison, George (gold prospector) 225
Harrison, William Henry 57
Heidi 202
Heisenberg, Werner 100
Henry I 153
Henry II 2, 70
Henry VIII 49
Henry, Prince of Prussia 35–6
Heroin, creation of 125
Herschel, William 117
Heston, Charlton 174
High Sierra 172

Hill, Glenallen (baseball player) 210
Hillary, Edmund 17
Hiroshima, nuclear attack on 100
Hitler, Adolf 16, 34–6, 80–5, 89–90, 95, 101
Hoffman, Dustin 175
Holdsworth, Dean (footballer) 209
Holiday Inn, origin of name 228
Hollerith, Herman (inventor) 157–8
Holloshaza (Hungary) 104
Hollywood, origin of 169
Home, (Lord) Alec Douglas- 29
Honduras 115–6
Horch, August 149
Horse racing 203
House of Commons 21, 25–7
Hubble space telescope 134
Huddersfield FC 207
Hudson, Rock 177
Hughes, Charles Evans 43
Hundred Years' War 70
Hunt, Walter (inventor) 119
Hussein, Saddam 104–5

IBM 151, 158
Ice cream, influence of 191
I Claudius 185
India (British Raj) 8
India, legal delays 220–1